EASY HOLIDAY ITALIAN

BY ANGIE BRANAES

Easy Holiday Italian

Seconda Casa - Easy Italian for Living Like a Local

ANGIE BRANAES

EASY HOLIDAY ITALIAN

ENGLISH STORY WITH ITALIAN DIALOGUE FOR BEGINNERS

First Edition, 2025

Published by CiaoHello

Cover design by Angie Branaes

This is a work of fiction. Any resemblance to actual persons, businesses, places, events, and brands is purely coincidental.

A CIP catalogue record for this book is available from the British Library.

ISBN: 978-1-0683352-0-4

For my parents, who have taken me on holidays in Italy for as long as I can remember, and for my husband, who makes every trip an adventure.

Table of Contents

Welcome 1

How to Read This Book 2

Capitolo 1: First Day in Italy 3

Capitolo 2: At the Seaside 40

Capitolo 3: Staying at a Tuscan Agriturismo 69

Capitolo 4: Exploring Tuscany 92

Capitolo 5: Visiting Florence 117

Capitolo 6: Last Day in Italy 158

Before You Go 159

About the Author 161

Frequently Used Expressions 162

Italian Grammar Cheat Sheet 169

Useful Italian Verbs 185

Vocabulary 190

Welcome

Ciao!

Easy Holiday Italian takes you on a typical holiday in Italy, teaching you simple phrases and conversations along the way. Soon, you'll confidently order a *caffè* at the local café, ask for sizes while out shopping, and enjoy wine tasting at a local vineyard.

I wrote *Easy Holiday Italian* because I wanted create a fun and casual read that helps you learn Italian while relaxing on holiday, or to get you excited for your upcoming holiday! In Italy, you'll likely meet several locals who don't speak English. Knowing some essential Italian phrases will get you far, and make your holiday more immersive and enjoyable.

Buona vacanza,
Angie Branaes

How to Read This Book

Top tip: Don't look up every word on the first read!

Easy Holiday Italian helps you learn the Italian you need on holiday by reading for fun. By reading an Italian story, you will naturally absorb vocabulary and internalize grammar, without feeling like you are studying.

Designed for complete beginners, *Easy Holiday Italian* features simple language and common holiday conversations, with repetition to help you remember the words you'll need to use often.

To make it easy to understand what's happening, only the dialogue with locals is in Italian. The story and explanations are in English. After reading each Italian conversation a few times, try practicing out loud — either on your own or with a partner.

Enjoy the process and don't hesitate to read the book multiple times. You will notice your Italian improving on each re-read. Over time, you will feel more comfortable speaking Italian. Try ordering in Italian the next time you're at a restaurant in Italy!

~ CAPITOLO 1 ~

First Day in Italy

It's the first day of Maria and Sarah's Italian holiday. During their trip, they will visit a beautiful seaside town, stay at a traditional Tuscan agriturismo, and explore the sights in Florence. Excited for their adventure, they look forward to discovering the country, tasting the local food, and experiencing Italian culture.

Arriving in Italy

Maria and Sarah have just landed in Italy for their holiday. Sarah is especially excited, as it's her first time in Italy. Maria has been to Italy before, and speaks a bit of Italian. They have just picked up their luggage and are exiting the airport into a hot and sunny Italian summer day.

Maria: Welcome to Italy! You're going to love it here.

Sarah: I'm so excited, I can't wait to try the food, see the sights, and swim in the sea!

Maria: Soon we will be at the hotel, and then we can start exploring. I'll grab us a taxi.

They walk up to the first taxi at the taxi stand. Maria, who knows a bit of Italian, says hello to the taxi driver and asks how much it costs to go to the Grand Hotel.

Maria: Buongiorno!

Taxi Driver: Buongiorno!

Maria: Quanto costa un taxi per il Grand Hotel?

Taxi Driver: Costa circa trenta euro. Ho il tassametro.

Maria: Va bene, prendiamo il taxi.

The taxi driver helps them load their luggage into the taxi, and they get in.

Sarah: I had no idea you spoke such good Italian!

Maria: I go to Italy every year and I have some Italian family, so I speak conversational Italian.

Sarah: Then maybe you can teach me a bit while we're here?

Maria: Of course! I'll do my best to explain everything.

Sarah: Thanks! What did you say to the taxi driver just before we got in?

Maria: I said *buongiorno*, which is how you politely say hello to someone in Italian during the day. It literally translates to good day. Then I asked him how much it would cost to get to the Grand Hotel.

Sarah: What did he say?

Maria: He said it would cost about thirty euro. He has a taxi meter. I told him that it's fine and we will take the taxi.

Sarah: Ah ok, thank you for explaining!

Maria: Happy to help!

The taxi drives into a charming seaside town. Colourful houses dot the hillside in shades of yellows, reds and oranges. The town has a tight cluster of pastel houses spreading from the sea and up towards the hill. There is a beautiful promenade next to the beach, filled with people in vibrant summer clothes going for walks. On the way to their hotel, they pass many cute shops, restaurants and cafes.

Sarah: Wow, the town is stunning. I can't wait to explore it!

The taxi driver pulls up in front of the Grand Hotel. It's a magnificent hotel that looks like it was built in the early 1900s.

Taxi Driver: Ecco qui. In totale sono trenta euro.

Maria: Grazie. Pago con la carta.

Taxi Driver: Ottimo. Buona vacanza!

Maria turns to Sarah and explains what just happened.

Maria: Our trip cost thirty euros in the end. I paid with my card. The taxi driver wished us a good holiday, which is nice of him. *Grazie* is how you say thank you in Italian by the way.

Sarah: *Grazie* for explaining!

Maria and Sarah get out of the taxi and grab their luggage. They walk into the hotel, ready to start their Italian holiday.

Checking in to the hotel

The lobby of the Grand Hotel is beautiful, with checkered marble floors, a tall ceiling and a large reception desk. Maria and Sarah briefly stop to marvel at the architecture before going over to the reception desk to check in. They are welcomed to the hotel by a female receptionist with brown hair in a bun, and a big smile on her face.

Receptionist: Benvenuti al Grand Hotel!

Maria: Buongiorno!

Sarah: Buongiorno!

Receptionist: Buongiorno, come posso aiutarvi?

Maria: Ho una prenotazione per una camera con due letti singoli per due notti.

Receptionist: Certo. Mi servono il nome e i vostri documenti d'identità, per favore.

Maria: Mi chiamo Maria Bianchi.

Maria tells the receptionist her name, then turns to Sarah to explain.

Maria: I told the receptionist we've reserved a room with two beds for two nights. She asked for our names and IDs. Could you give me your passport?

Sarah: Here you go.

Maria hands their passports to the receptionist.

Maria: Ecco i passaporti.

Receptionist: Grazie. Un momento, per favore.

The receptionist checks their passports, then hands them back together with the key to their room.

Receptionist: Ecco i passaporti e la chiave della camera duecentocinque. La vostra camera è al secondo piano.

Maria takes the key from the receptionist, and turns to Sarah to explain.

Maria: I've just checked us in. We're in room 205, which is on the second floor.

Sarah: Great! Let's drop our bags in the room, then go get something to eat and explore the town.

They get up to their room and put their bags down by the door. Sarah walks over to the window and looks out across the town. When she speaks, she sounds disappointed.

Sarah: Oh no, we didn't get a room with a sea view. I really wanted to have a view of the sea.

Maria: Let's go ask if we can change rooms.

They go back down to the reception again. Maria smiles at the receptionist and nicely asks her if they can change rooms to one with a sea view.

Maria: Buongiorno. Scusi, possiamo cambiare camera? La nostra camera non ha la vista sul mare. Vogliamo una camera con la vista sul mare, se possibile.

Receptionist: Sì, una camera con la vista sul mare è disponibile. Ecco qui le chiave della camera trecentodieci.

Maria: Grazie mille! Ecco qui le chiave della camera duecentocinque.

Maria exchanges keys with the receptionist, then looks jubilant as she turns to Sarah.

Maria: They gave us a room with a sea view! Our new room is 310. Let's go check it out!

Sarah and Maria go drop their bags in their new room. They pause in front of the window to enjoy the splendid view of the sun shining on the sea.

Sarah: What a beautiful view!

Maria: *Bellissima*, as they say here.

A few moments later, they leave the hotel to get a bite to eat and go explore the town.

Visiting a cafe

While exploring the charming streets outside their hotel, Maria and Sarah discover a cute cafe with a view of the ocean. Outdoors seating spills across the pavement, and a green and white striped awning provides shade from the strong summer sunshine. Most of the tables are full, with customers enjoying coffees and pastries while chatting and watching people go by. The women decide to stop at the cafe to get a coffee and something small to eat.

Stepping inside the cafe, they eagerly approach the pastry filled counter to see what's available. There is a wide assortment of fresh sandwiches, sweet cakes, and fluffy Italian croissants to choose from.

Sarah: Oh look at all the delicious food! I'd love to have the croissant with ham and cheese in it, and a cappuccino. Can you order that for me?

Maria: Yes, happy to. I'll also get myself an espresso and a sandwich with cured ham.

Maria turns to the smiling woman at the counter to place their order.

Donna: Buongiorno! Cosa desiderate?

Maria: Buongiorno! Vorrei un caffè e un panino con prosciutto crudo, per favore. Lei invece prende un cappuccino e una brioche salata con prosciutto e formaggio. Vorrei anche due bottiglie d'acqua naturale.

Donna: Certo. In tutto sono dieci euro.

Maria: Grazie. Pago con la carta.

Maria pays with her card.

The woman makes their coffees and puts them on the counter. She puts their plates of food and two bottles of still water next to it. Sarah takes the drinks outside and finds a table, and Maria follows with the ham and cheese croissant and the sandwich. They sit down and enjoy their food while watching people go by.

Sarah: How come you call your espresso just *caffè* and they get it?

Maria: In Italy an espresso is the standard size of coffee. So you can just say *caffè* or *caffè normale* to get an espresso.

Sarah: Oh, I see. My cappuccino is delicious, so I might just stick with that.

Maria: I'm glad you like it. You can stick with your cappuccino, but you should know that Italians mainly drink cappuccino for breakfast. You might get some comments if you order it later in the day.

Sarah: Oh I didn't know that, thanks for the tip! I love learning about local customs.

Maria: I'll let you know if we come across any other Italian customs you should know about. After we finish our food, let's go explore the town!

They slowly finish their coffees and food while chatting about everything they want to do on their holiday. The view of the sun sparkling on the ocean and of people leisurely walking by is relaxing, leading them to have a longer breakfast than they would usually have at home.

Exploring the seaside town

Having leisurely enjoyed some light refreshments at a local cafe, Maria and Sarah feel energised after their long flight. They are ready to explore the small seaside town they just arrived in.

They start out by going for a stroll to take in the sights. Their route takes them along the beachfront promenade, before they follow a sign to the *centro storico*, taking them away from the sea and into the historic old town. In the *centro storico* they wind through narrow *strade* of colourful houses. Some of the *strade* have tiny shops selling local foods, clothes, and toys.

Sarah: I love all the local shops. There are so many products I've never seen before, and I've hardly heard of any of these brands.

Maria: Yeah, it's an amazing selection of local crafts here in the *centro storico*, and often in Italian towns in general. I especially love the shoe and leather shops for their quality materials and craftsmanship. And for those that like shopping on holiday, you can never go wrong with vibrant, Italian summer clothes!

They pass by an old, catholic church and take a look inside. There they find the walls covered in classical artwork, decorative marble pillars, and a ceiling reaching for the sky with intricate frescoes painted onto it.

Sarah: Wow, I've never seen a church like this before! Look at all the exquisite detail and decoration.

Maria: *Chiese cattoliche* in the mediterranean are something else. I find that the best art galleries are often the *chiese* actually, as they all have their own historic artworks on display, so I rarely go to the museums. This one is just a local *chiesa*, wait until you see the magnificent *cattedrale* found in some of the larger cities!

Sarah: I'd love to see the art in some more churches while we're here.

They make their way to the town square, a charming space overlooking the sea. At the center stands a small fountain. Across from the fountain, a *gelateria* tempts visitors with colorful displays of *gelato*. Restaurants with outdoor seating line the square, their tables offering a view of the sea and the lively atmosphere.

Sarah: How cute is this! I love that it's possible to eat dinner outdoors in the square.

Maria: Yes, it's lovely. Looks like we found the main *piazza* of the town! A *piazza* is a large, open square in a town. At night, it will probably be filled with people eating at the restaurants, and kids playing in the piazza.

Sarah: That sounds really atmospheric. Let's come back and have dinner here tonight.

Sarah spots a popular *gelateria* at the opposite side of the square to them, with a small queue, and happy kids eating *gelato*.

Sarah: Look, a *gelateria*! Let's go check it out.

Visiting the gelateria

The gelateria in the piazza features a vibrant display of gelato, with flavors in every color of the rainbow. Rows of tubs are piled high with creamy scoops, each one topped with fresh fruit, chocolate shavings, or crunchy nuts to hint at the flavor.

Maria: Let's get some gelato to cool down. It's so hot today.

Sarah: Yes, I can't wait to try real Italian gelato.

The women walk into the gelateria to take a closer look at the flavours in the counter. Sarah points at some of the flavours and asks Maria what they are.

Sarah: What is this red one that says *fragola*?

Maria: It's strawberry. Looks like sorbet. Usually a fruit flavour is a *sorbetto*, which means there's no milk in it.

Sarah: The *fragola* looks nice. What are these other *sorbetti*? There is a pink *lampone*, a white *limone* and a purple *frutti di bosco*.

Maria: The pink *lampone* is raspberry. The white *limone* is lemon, which goes great with *cioccolato* by the way. The purple *frutti di bosco* is the fruit of the forest. I often like pairing a *sorbetto* with a normal gelato flavour, for a nice mix of creamy and fresh. The smallest gelato you can get is usually two flavours, so it's fun to try two very different tastes and textures.

Sarah: Pairing a *sorbetto* with normal gelato sounds like a great idea! In that case, what do these other gelato flavours like *nocciola*, *crema*, and *amarena* mean?

Maria: *Nocciola* sounds like it's just nuts, but it specifically means hazelnuts in Italian. *Amarena* is sour, black cherries mixed into plain gelato. *Crema* is as simple as a gelato can get, just eggs, sugar and milk – often with a little orange zest for added depth of flavour. It's one of the most popular gelato flavours in Italy, similar to how we'd buy vanilla ice cream by default back home.

Sarah: Thank you for explaining. I'd love to try your recommendation to mix a *sorbetto* with a gelato flavour. I think I'll have *limone* and *cioccolato*.

Maria: Great! Do you want to try to order that yourself? Say *cono* if you want an ice cream cone, or *coppetta* if you want a small paper cup. It's *due gusti* for two flavours, and you just say the flavour after. I'll demonstrate by going first.

Maria turns to the woman behind the gelato counter to place her order.

Donna: Buongiorno. Cono o coppetta?

Maria: Buongiorno. Un cono piccolo con due gusti, crema e lampone.

The woman takes a small cone and fills it with one scoop of *crema* gelato and one scoop of raspberry *sorbetto*. She hands it to Maria.

Donna: Ecco qui.

Maria asks if she can have a spoon for her gelato.

Maria: Scusi, posso avere un cucchiaino, per favore?

The woman hands Maria a small, yellow plastic spoon. She then turns to Sarah and asks what she wants.

Donna: Cono o coppetta?

Sarah: Coppetta. Con due gusti, limone e cioccolato.

The *donna* takes a small *coppetta* paper cup for the gelato, and fills it with a scoop of lemon *sorbetto* and a scoop of chocolate gelato. She puts a pink plastic spoon in it and hands it to Sarah.

Donna: Ecco. In totale sono cinque euro.

Maria hands the *donna* five euros.

Maria: Ecco i soldi. Arrivederci!

Donna: Arrivederci!

Maria and Sarah exit the shop and walk through the piazza towards the seafront promenade while enjoying their gelatos.

Sarah: So what is *piccolo* anyway? I heard you say *un cono piccolo* to the gelato woman.

Maria: Piccolo means small. I wanted a small sized ice cream cone. If you want the large one, you can use the word *grande*, which means big. *Un cono grande*.

Sarah: I'll try that next time. Thank you for explaining.

They finish their gelatos and continue their leisurely stroll along the promenade, enjoying the view of the boats bobbing in the distance, children playing in the water, and people relaxing on the beach.

Exploring the food shops

After having had a nice stroll along the seafront promenade and finished their gelatos, it's time to continue exploring. Heading back into town from the seafront, they walk down a street that has many local food shops.

The first shop they pass is a fruit vendor, who has more of his vibrant produce in large baskets outside his store than inside. There are piles of oranges, giant lemons with the leaves still attached, juicy watermelon quarters, and plenty of colourful tomato varieties.

Sarah: Look at all the fruit and vegetables outside this store! I've never seen a tomato this big, or *pomodoro* as the sign says.

Maria: Yes, you can get an amazing selection of fresh fruit and vegetables in Italy, including many varieties we don't get at home. The fruit and vegetable shops like this one are really common, and it's where most people buy their vegetables. You'll find at least one in every town, and usually a few at the local markets too. In Italian they're called *fruttivendolo*.

Sarah: Fruttivendolo. Thanks! How would I say *Let's go to the fruit and vegetable shop* in Italian?

Maria: Andiamo dal fruttivendolo.

Sarah: *Andiamo dal fruttivendolo*. Thanks! What is *andiamo*?

Maria: Andiamo is the "we" form of the verb "to go". You can look it up under *andare* in your dictionary. In Italian they conjugate the verb depending on who is doing the action, so it's different if I do something, if you do it, if I say that Sarah is doing something, or if we're doing it together. Most "we" forms end in *-iamo*, so you'll learn to recognise it fast.

Sarah: Wow that's a lot to keep track of!

Maria: Yes, it can be a lot at first, but it's pretty easy when you get used to it. Talking about food, say you wanted to use the right form of *mangiare*, which means to eat. If I'm eating, it's *io mangio*, if I say you're eating it's *tu mangi*, and if she's eating you say *lei mangia*. Most verbs that end in *-are* follow this pattern. So the neat thing is that I can say *mangi* without the *tu* in front and you will still understand that I'm talking about you eating something. The gotcha is that if you use the wrong verb ending, people can be confused about who you're talking about.

Sarah: Ah that's kind of neat, but also seems error prone for beginners.

Maria: Yes, I recommend practicing the most common verbs a bit to get them right.

Maria and Sarah continue down the quaint street, passing by more food shops. Sarah stops to look in through the window of the bakery. The walls are lined with fresh bread, and the counter has a giant focaccia, as well as several types of flavoured focaccia with toppings like sun dried tomatoes and rosemary. Next to the till are jars of several different types of biscuits.

Sarah: The focaccia looks delicious. What do you call bread in Italian?

Maria: In Italian bread is called *pane*, and a shop that sells bread is called a *panetteria*. If you're looking for a loaf of bread, you'd often refer to it as *pagnotta*, but they'll get it if you just say *un pane* too. The bread is best fresh, so you'd ideally go to the baker every morning to get it.

Sarah: I'd be up for a daily trip to the *panetteria*. Today I would love to try some real Italian focaccia.

Maria: *Proviamo*! Let's try!

Maria goes into the bakery, with Sarah following closely behind. Upon entering, they are met with the delicious smell of freshly baked bread. They walk up to the counter, where Maria orders from the baker, an elderly man that looks friendly.

Panettiere: Buongiorno!

Maria: Buongiorno! Vorrei un pezzo di focaccia, per favore.

Panettiere: Quale pezzo di focaccia desidera?

The baker asks which piece focaccia Maria would like to have, as there are many different types and pieces in the counter.

Maria: Questa focaccia genovese, per favore.

Maria skips over the special varieties with toppings like sun-dried tomatoes, olives, rosemary, or tomato and cheese. She points to a plain focaccia genovese with salt and olive oil.

To confirm that he has the right piece, the baker points at the same piece as Maria indicated from the other side of the counter.

Panettiere: Questo?

Maria: Sì, grazie.

The baker takes the piece of focaccia Maria pointed to, puts it into a small paper bag, and hands it to her.

Panettiere: Ecco qui. Viene un euro.

Maria: Grazie. Ecco a lei.

Maria pays, then gives the bag with the focaccia to Sarah.

Maria: *Ecco.* Here is your piece of focaccia. It was just one euro.

Sarah: Wow, that's so cheap! I'll have to come back here every day to try all the different kinds of bread.

Maria: We should. It's a delicious way to learn the names for the different types of bread and cakes.

Sarah: What does *ecco* mean by the way? I hear you and the Italians say it all the time.

Maria: *Ecco* means here, as in here you go or here it is.

Sarah: What does it mean when they say *ecco qui* or *ecco a lei* then?

Maria: *Ecco a lei* is the polite way to say here you go. The *qui* just emphasises that it's here. Some version of *ecco* is often used when handing over something, but not always.

Sarah eats her fresh focaccia as they continue down the street. As they walk, Maria points at more of the local shops and explains what they are. They pass by a fishmonger, who has a giant counter of fresh fish in his store.

Maria: In Italian towns there are often specialty shops for every kind of fresh produce. This shop here that sells fresh fish is called the *pescheria*.

Next to the *pescheria* is a butcher's shop with two large counters of fresh meat.

Maria: The butcher's shop is called the *macelleria*. The *macelleria* only sells fresh, raw meat. It's perfect if you want to buy chicken or steak.

Sarah: Do they also sell Parma ham?

Maria: No, if you're looking for cured meats like salami or *prosciutto di Parma*, you'd go to the *salumeria*.

Sarah: Where can I get cheese?

Maria: If you're looking for cheese, you can find it at the *formaggeria*. To keep it simple, I usually just get my cured meats and cheeses when I go to the grocery store, which is either a tiny local *alimentari* food shop or a small *supermercato*. In those shops you can go up to the *banco dei formaggi* or *banco dei salumi* to get the products you want sliced by weight. Remarkably, even the smallest shops usually have these counters.

Sarah: There are so many different shops, I look forward to trying them all on our holiday. I can't wait to pick up lots of *salumi* and *formaggi* to try!

Maria: Yes, I can't wait to eat our way through Italy!

Sarah: You've mentioned a lot of smaller shops, do they not have big supermarkets in Italy?

Maria: Yes, they do. An *ipermercato* is a giant supermarket that is usually in a mall or outside the small town centres. They have large selections of fresh and cured meats, cheeses, fresh fish, vegetables, and wine.

Sarah: Sounds like you're spoiled for choice when it comes to grocery shopping in Italy!

Maria: You really are!

The two friends continue walking down the street, exploring the local shops.

The midday break

Walking around town towards the end of the lunch period, Maria and Sarah notice that most of the shops are closing.

Sarah: 1pm seems early to close up shop for the day. How come all the shops are just open for half the day?

Maria: It's time for the midday break, or *la pausa* as they call it here. It's similar to the siesta in Spain. As it's really hot during the day, shops usually close from lunchtime to 4pm in the afternoon. People go for a long lunch, maybe cool down with a swim, and have a nap. Most shops then re-open at 4pm.

Sarah: Oh that's such an interesting and different way of doing things. It must be really nice to have that afternoon break to enjoy the nicest hours of the day.

Maria: Yes, it's nice. But as a tourist you really have to remember that you can't get any errands done in the afternoon! I often forget, and I'm then met with closed shops.

Sarah: Duly noted. Errands are for mornings.

They sit down on a bench and enjoy the view of the sea.

Going for *aperitivo*

Maria and Sarah are still out exploring town when the sun slowly starts to set. It's about six o'clock in the evening, and many cafes and restaurants are buzzing with people enjoying Aperol Spritzes and nibbles.

Maria: Looks like it's finally *aperitivo* time!

Sarah: What's *aperitivo*?

Maria: Since dinner isn't until about eight in the evening, *aperitivo* is a social pre-dinner appetizer that takes place around six, when you still get some evening sun. It's a laid-back way to unwind after work or a long day at the beach while enjoying light refreshments. Aperol or Campari Spritz is the classic drink of choice, and there are snacks and nibbles served on the side.

Sarah: That sounds amazing! Let's find a bar and have *aperitivo*.

They see a free table at a bar with a view of the sea and the sunset. The low sun is bathing the guests and their drinks in warm rays, making their orange spritzes practically glow fire red. After they sit down, the waiter comes over with menus.

Cameriere: Buonasera!

Maria: Buonasera. Due Aperol Spritz, per favore.

Cameriere: Certo. Arrivo subito.

The waiter takes their order and disappears back inside.

Sarah: So if *buongiorno* means good day, does *buonasera* mean good evening?

Maria: Yes, that's correct. *Giorno* means day, and *sera* means evening.

A short while later the waiter returns with two large wine glasses, filled to the brim with red-orange Aperol Spritz over ice cubes, and decorated with a slice of orange. He also gives them a tray of snacks, including crisps, salted peanuts, small sandwiches, and olives.

Cameriere: Ecco i vostri spritz e gli stuzzichini. Ci sono olive, patatine, arachidi salate e tramezzini.

Maria: Grazie mille!

Sarah: Oh wow, this looks delicious! Cheers!

Maria: *Salute*, as they say in Italy.

Sarah: Salute!

They slowly enjoy their snacks and drinks while watching the sunset from their table at the bar. When the last rays of the sun dip below the ocean, they go to find a restaurant for dinner.

Dinner in the *piazza*

It's eight o'clock in the evening, making it dinner time in Italy. Maria and Sarah are hungry after a long day of travelling to Italy and exploring the seaside town they are staying in.

Sarah: I'm starving. Let's go get dinner at one of the restaurants in the town *piazza*.

Maria: Great idea. Let's walk over.

The women walk over to the *piazza*. The town is lively, with lots of people out for walks. The shops are open, and colourful clothes, ceramics, and shoes are on display outside.

When they get to the *piazza* they see that it's bustling. Kids are running around and playing in the square. The restaurants are quickly filling up with happy diners, and delicious smells of Italian foods are wafting across the *piazza*.

Sarah stops outside a pizzeria.

Sarah: Can we get pizza? I really want to try real Italian pizza!

Maria: Sure! I'll ask if they have a table for two.

Maria walks into the restaurant and asks a waiter if they have a table.

Maria: Buonasera. Posso avere un tavolo per due persone, per favore.

Cameriere: Buonasera. Avete una prenotazione?

Maria: No, non abbiamo una prenotazione.

Cameriere: Non importa. Venite con me.

The waiter takes them to a table in the outdoors section of the restaurant with a view of the *piazza*. He hands them menus.

Cameriere: Cosa desiderate da bere?

Maria: Dell'acqua frizzante, per favore.

Cameriere: Va bene, ritorno subito.

A few minutes later the waiter returns to their table with a bottle of sparkling water. He proceeds to take their order.

Cameriere: Che cosa prendete?

Sarah: Per me, una pizza con i peperoni.

Maria laughs.

Maria: I'm guessing you want a pizza with pepperoni, not the vegetable peppers? In Italian, *peperoni* translates to bell peppers. At a typical pizzeria, the closest pizza to a classic pepperoni pizza is usually the Diavola. It comes with spicy salami, and a drizzle of chilli oil or other spicy toppings. I see one here on the menu.

Sarah: OK, I'll have the Diavola.

Maria turns to the waiter.

Maria: Lei vuole una pizza alla Diavola, per favore. Io invece vorrei una pizza Capricciosa e una bottiglia di vino rosso della casa.

Cameriere: Va bene.

The waiter walks off with their order, and Maria turns back to Sarah.

Maria: I ordered you a pizza alla Diavola. I'm having the Capricciosa, which has ham, mushrooms, olives and artichokes on it. I also got us a bottle of the house red.

Sarah: Sounds great, thank you for saving me from getting a pizza with only bell peppers on top!

Maria: Happy to help!

Sarah: I'm guessing *lei* means she, from how you ordered?

Maria: Yes, *lei* means both she and her. And in Italian *lei* is also used when people are being polite, as they then talk to you in third person. The formal version takes a bit of time to get used to.

Sarah: That's very good to know. What would you use for him?

Maria: You say *lui*. So it's *lui* for he, *lei* for she, and *lei* when you are being polite.

Sarah: Thanks for summarising.

A few minutes later the waiter returns with the pizzas and the wine.

Cameriere: Ecco qui la pizza alla Diavola, la pizza Capricciosa e il vino rosso della casa.

Maria: Grazie mille!

While eating, the women chat about their day and watch the activity in the square. Kids are running around and playing on their own. There is a queue for the gelateria. Street vendors selling light-up toys in the piazza, hoping to draw the eye of eager kids.

When they have finished eating their pizzas, the waiter comes over to take their plates.

Cameriere: Posso?

Maria: Sì, grazie.

The waiter leaves with their finished plates.

Sarah: What does *posso* mean?

Maria: When the waiter asks to take your finished plates, they typically say *posso*, which means "can I?". You'll hear it a lot when you're in Italy, as it's used for everything, from the waiter asking to take your plates at a restaurant, to you asking if you can try on some clothes in a shop. It's from the verb *potere*.

Sarah: Thanks for explaining! I'm too full for dessert, should we ask for the bill?

Maria: Yes, I'll do that now.

Maria makes a payment gesture to the waiter by drawing a signature in the air, and asks for the bill.

Maria: Il conto, per favore.

A moment later, the waiter brings the bill over to the table.

Maria: Grazie. Pago con la carta di credito.

Maria pays for the bill by card, and they get up to leave.

Cameriere: Grazie, arrivederci!

They exit the restaurant, pausing outside while watching the buzzing nightlife and deciding what to do next.

Maria: How are you feeling? If you're tired, we can go back to the hotel. Otherwise we should make the most of the nightlife. We can go get a drink at a bar, get some more gelato, or go shopping.

Sarah: You can go shopping at night after dinner? Let's do that!

After dinner shopping

Maria and Sarah have just finished their first dinner in Italy. They have enjoyed eating outdoors on a balmy Italian evening with a front row view of the town piazza. They have been watching kids running around and playing, well dressed adults strolling with gelatos, and now see the several shops reopening for the evening.

Sarah: How come shops reopen after dinner? I've never seen shops open this late before.

Maria: In the high season in summer shops typically reopen after dinner. Since it's so hot during the day, after dinner is when everyone is out walking around town and enjoying the balmy temperature and lively atmosphere. Even kids are allowed to stay up late and play outside.

Sarah: That's amazing! Come on, let's go check out the shops!

The women join the crowd walking through the shopping streets.

Sarah stops at one of the first shops they get to. Like many other shops on the street, it has its products on display outside. Sarah browses through a rack of colourful summer dresses.

Sarah: Look at these vibrant summer dresses! I can't believe they can just hang outside the shop on the street. I love it. Let's go try some on.

Sarah grabs three dresses off the rack. They have patterns in different colours, one is red, one is blue and one is green. As they enter the shop, Maria asks the shop assistant if Sarah can try on the dresses.

Maria: Buonasera! Può provare questi vestiti?

Commessa: Buonasera. Certo! Il camerino è lì.

The shop assistant points at the fitting room in the corner of the shop.

Sarah goes into the fitting room and tries on the dresses.

Sarah: Oh no, the dresses are a bit small. Can you ask her if she has a larger size?

Maria: Yeah, Italian sizes are deceptively small. They usually run about two sizes smaller than other European sizes. I'll ask for a larger size.

Maria takes the dresses from Sarah and turns to the shop assistant.

Maria: Questi vestiti sono troppo piccoli per lei. Può provare una taglia più grande?

Commessa: Certo. Un momento.

The shop assistant finds the dresses in larger sizes.

Commessa: Allora. Ecco qui il vestito rosso e il vestito verde in una taglia più grande. Non ho il vestito blu in una taglia più grande.

Maria: Grazie!

Maria takes the two larger dresses from the shop assistant and hands them to Sarah in the fitting room.

Maria: Here are the red and the green dresses in bigger sizes. Unfortunately she didn't have the blue dress in a bigger size.

Sarah: Thanks!

Sarah tries on both dresses and shows Maria.

Sarah I think I like the red dress better, can you ask how much it is?

Maria: Quanto costa il vestito rosso?

Commessa: Costa venti euro. Sta benissimo con il vestito rosso, è una scelta perfetta!

Maria: She says the dress is twenty euro, and that you look great in it so it's the perfect choice.

Sarah: *Grazie mille!* I'll take it.

Maria: Lo prendo. Posso pagare con la carta?

Commessa: Certo. Ecco il POS.

Sarah pays by card, and the shop assistant hands her the bag with her new dress while wishing her a good evening.

Sarah: Grazie.

Commessa: Buona serata.

They exit the shop, and happily continue browsing the stores.

The forgotten toothbrush

It's late and Maria and Sarah are exhausted after a long, but amazing, first day in Italy. They are back in their room and getting ready to go to bed. Sarah is admiring the view of the quiet ocean and the starry night through their window. Maria is in the bathroom doing her night time routine.

Sarah: Thank you again for successfully swapping our room to one with a view of the ocean. The view is absolutely stunning. You can see the stars and the moon so clearly, it's even reflecting in the ocean. Come look.

Maria: I'll come in a moment, I just need to brush my teeth.

Sarah admires the view for a moment longer, before she hears Maria exclaim something from the bathroom.

Maria: Oh no, I forgot to pack my toothbrush and toothpaste!

Sarah: Hotels usually have that, isn't there any in the bathroom?

Maria: No, I can only see shower gels and cotton pads here.

Sarah: Why don't you call down to reception and ask if they can bring a toothbrush and some toothpaste up to you?

Maria: That's a great idea. I'll give them a call now.

Maria finds the phone on her nightstand and calls down to reception for a toothbrush and toothpaste.

Receptionist: Pronto.

Maria: Buonasera. Ho dimenticato lo spazzolino e il dentifricio. Li avete?

Receptionist: Sì. Aspetti un momento. Le porto lo spazzolino e il dentifricio in camera.

Five minutes later, there is a soft knock on the door. Maria opens it, and finds the receptionist outside with a pack containing a toothbrush and a small toothpaste.

Receptionist: Buonasera. Ecco lo spazzolino e il dentifricio.

Maria: Grazie mille! Buona notte!

Maria takes the *spazzolino* and *dentifricio* that the receptionist hands her, and wishes the receptionist good night. She can now brush her teeth and go to bed.

~ CAPITOLO 2 ~

At the Seaside

First breakfast in Italy

It's the start of a beautiful day by the Italian seaside. The sun is shining from a bright, blue sky and it's already warm outside. Maria and Sarah have just left their hotel to grab breakfast at a local cafe, before heading to the beach to soak up the sun.

Exiting the hotel, they quickly spot a cute cafe nearby that has outdoor seating with a view of the sea. They are in luck, as a few tables are still unoccupied. They grab a free table outdoors, and soon a friendly waitress comes over to take their order.

Cameriera: Buongiorno! Che cosa prendete per colazione?

Maria: Due cappucci, due cornetti e dell'acqua naturale, per favore.

Cameriera: Perfetto, arrivo subito.

Maria turns to Sarah to explain as the waitress disappears inside.

Maria: I've ordered us a typical Italian breakfast, or *colazione* as it's called here. We have cappuccinos, Italian croissants which are called *cornetto*s, and some still water. Breakfast in Italy is typically sweet with just some pastries or cakes.

Sarah: I can get on board with cakes for breakfast! How come you call it *cappucci* when it's multiple cappuccinos but *cappuccino* when it's just one?

Maria: In Italian the ending changes depending on whether we're talking about a singular item or multiple items. So if it ends in an -o as a singular item, it ends in an -i as plural items. So it's technically one *cappuccino, due cappuccini*, but you'll notice most cafes use the colloquial shorthand *cappucci*.

Sarah: Got it, thank you for explaining. What do you do with words that don't end in an -o, like pizza?

Maria: For words that end in an -a, you'll change the ending to an -e. So it's *una pizza, due pizze*. To get the articles right, it's worth remembering that most words ending in -o are masculine and most words ending in -a are feminine.

Sarah: So does that mean that the classic sandwich panini is actually plural, and it should be *panino* when we refer to a single sandwich?

Maria: Yes, that's correct. In Italy you ask for a *panino* if you want a single sandwich, and *panini* if you want multiple sandwiches.

At that moment the smiling waitress returns with their *cappuccis*, *cornettis* and *acqua naturale.*

Cameriera Ecco. Buon appetito!

Sarah: Grazie!

Sarah takes a bite of her *cornetto*, and smiles.

Sarah: These Italian *cornettos* are delicious. They are so fluffy, almost like a brioche. Very different from the typical French croissant I'm used to.

Maria: I love them too. You really can't beat cakes for breakfast to feel like you're on holiday! Many places in Northern Italy call the *cornetto* brioche actually, especially if they are filled with something savoury. Then they're often referred to as *brioche salate.* If they have sweet fillings, you often get them with cream as *cornetto alla crema*, with jam as *cornetto alla marmellata*, or with chocolate as *cornetto al cioccolato.*

Sarah: Tomorrow we're having *cornetti* with sweet fillings. I want to try a *cornetto alla crema*, I've never had that before.

Maria: Sounds like a plan!

The women enjoy their breakfast in the sun, excited to soon be heading for the beach.

Buying beach gear

It's a hot and sunny summer day in Italy. Sarah and Maria are planning on spending the day on the beach, but first they need to buy some beach essentials they did not bring with them.

On their way to the beach they come across a store selling all sorts of beach gear. Outside the store there are large inflatable pool toys, like pink flamingos and beach balls. There is a shelf with magazines, towels in many colours, and lots of beach toys for all ages.

Maria: There are so many fun things we can get for the beach here! I'm going to get a straw hat, a red beach towel, and an inflatable beach ball.

Sarah: I need a beach towel, sunscreen, and a hat.

Sarah browses through the products outside the store and picks up a pink hat and a blue towel, but she can't find any sunscreen.

Sarah: I can't see any sunscreen, can you?

Maria: I'll ask the shop assistant if they have any.

Maria goes inside the store and greets the old man behind the till in Italian.

Commesso: Buongiorno.

Maria: Buongiorno. Avete una crema solare con fattore cinquanta?

Commesso: Sì. Ho questo modello. Va bene?

Maria: Grazie, va bene. Lo prendo.

Sarah comes over with her arms full of beach items. She puts them on the till next to Maria's items.

Sarah: Let's get these things too.

Maria: Sure!

Commesso: Allora. Due teli da mare, un cappello rosa, un cappello di paglia, una crema solare e una palla gonfiabile. In totale, cinquanta euro.

Sarah: Pago con la carta di credito.

Sarah pays by credit card and puts on her new pink hat.

Commesso: Grazie. Ecco qui le buste. Buona giornata!

The shop assistant hands them two bags of their new items, and they exit the store.

Maria: Well done for paying in Italian! You're picking up the language quickly!

Sarah: *Grazie mille!* Now let's go to the beach.

Buying snacks

On their way to the beach, Maria and Sarah come across a local fresh fruit and vegetable shop. Outside, there are baskets overflowing with juicy peaches, large tomatoes and fresh apricots.

Sarah: I'd love to get some fresh fruit for the beach, and I can't pass up an opportunity to see what real Italian fruits taste like. Let's pop into the *fruttivendolo* and get a selection.

They go over to the *fruttivendolo* and browse the large selection outside. Sarah picks some peaches and apricots, and practices the names she sees on the signs.

Sarah: Let's get some *pesche* and *albicocche* for the beach. Do you want anything else? The *arance*, *anguria* and *melone* look great too.

Maria: Great idea! I love fresh *albicocche*, at home you only get dried apricots. The *pesche* look really big and juicy. Let's skip the oranges, watermelon and melon. They are difficult to eat on the beach as we won't have a good way to slice them.

After buying fruits, they walk past a small kiosk that's not much more than a hole in the wall. There are some racks of crisps outside, a shelf of magazines, and plenty of soft drinks options.

Sarah: I'd love to get some salty crisps and some water.

They stop at the kiosk and Maria asks the vendor for the products.

Venditore: Buongiorno! Cosa desidera?

Maria: Buongiorno. Vorrei due bottiglie d'acqua naturale, e un sacchetto di patatine.

Venditore: Ecco qui. In totale sono quattro euro. Ti serve una busta?

Maria: No, grazie. Ecco quattro euro. Arrivederci!

Maria gives the kiosk vendor four euro. She then puts their products in her beach bag, and they head to the beach.

Visiting the private beach

The private beach near the Grand Hotel has a large sign that reads *Spiaggia Azzurra* on it. True to its name it's lined with azure blue and white striped umbrellas and azure blue beach beds. Maria and Sarah are walking over to the *Spiaggia Azzurra* to rent some beach beds, skipping the public beach that's quickly filling up with umbrellas and towels in all colours of the rainbow.

At the entrance to the beach is a small kiosk. It's manned by a tan man who looks like he spends all summer at the beach. Maria approaches the kiosk so she can rent two beach beds and an umbrella for the day.

Next to the kiosk window is a small sign that says *Noleggio* that lists the prices for the day rental of beach beds, deckchairs, umbrellas. It also lists the hourly rental of water toys. Sarah can see that a *lettino* is €10/*giorno*, a *sdraio* is €8/*giorno*, an *ombrellone* is €5/*giorno*, a *kayak* is €7/*ora* and a *SUP* is €8/*ora*.

Addetto: Buongiorno! Posso aiutarla?

Maria: Buongiorno. È possibile noleggiare due lettini e un ombrellone per oggi?

Addetto: Certo! Il costo è di venti euro per i lettini e cinque euro per l'ombrellone. In totale costano venticinque euro.

Maria: Avete qualcosa in prima fila?

Addetto: No, la prima fila è riservata per la stagione. Ma abbiamo due lettini in terza fila, lì a destra.

The man in the kiosk points to two beach chairs with an umbrella between them, located in the third row on the right side of the beach.

Maria: Va bene, li prendiamo. Posso pagare con la carta di credito?

Addetto: Sì, ecco il POS.

The kiosk attendant shows Maria the card machine, and she pays €25 by card for two beach loungers and an umbrella for the day. She then turns to Sarah to explain.

Maria: Follow me, I just rented the two beach chairs and the umbrella on the third row over on the right there. I tried to get something on the first row, but they told me those chairs are reserved for the season. In Italy, it's very common for people to reserve their beach chairs for the whole summer season.

Sarah: Sounds great. Let's go!

Sarah follows Maria over to the *lettini* they have rented for the day. They put their towels on the *lettini*, change into their swimsuits, and head straight to the water for a swim.

At the beach

The sea by the beach is calm, with any waves being caused by people playing in the water, swimmers doing their laps, or kayaks being taken out for short trips. The sun is high and hot, sparkling off the clear, blue ocean.

Maria and Sarah are swimming and playing in the water by the beach. Suddenly, a ball lands near them. It belongs to a group of friends who were having fun throwing the ball back and forth in the water a moment ago. One of the men shouts across and asks if they can pass the ball back to them.

Uomo: Scusa! Puoi passarmi la palla?

Maria: Certo. Ecco la palla!

Uomo: Grazie!

Maria throws the ball back to the group, and watches as they continue their game. A few minutes later, one of the women comes over to say hi.

Donna: Ciao, mi chiamo Laura. Voi come vi chiamate?

Maria: Ciao, mi chiamo Maria e lei si chiama Sarah.

Sarah: Ciao!

The woman tells them her name is Laura, and asks for their names. Maria and Sarah say hi back and tell her their names. Laura then asks if they are here on holiday.

Laura: Siete in vacanza qui?

Maria: Sì, siamo in vacanza qui per due giorni. Poi andiamo in Toscana, inclusa Firenze. Anche tu sei in vacanza qui?

Laura: Sì, ho una seconda casa qui per le vacanze. Vengo ogni estate. È un posto bellissimo, vero?

Maria: Sì, è meraviglioso. Ci piace tanto.

Maria explains that they are here on holiday for two days. Then they are going to Tuscany, followed by Florence. She asks if Laura is also here on holiday. Laura explains that she has a holiday home here that she visits every summer. They both agree that it's a beautiful place that they like very much.

Before she goes back to her friends, Laura recommends that they visit the trattoria in the main town piazza, as it's the best one in town.

Laura: Mentre siete qui, dovete andare alla trattoria nella piazza principale. È la migliore della città.

Maria: Davvero?

Laura: Il tiramisù è fantastico!

Maria: Grazie per il consiglio! Lo proveremo.

After having recommended that they try the tiramisu at the trattoria, Laura waves and walks back to her friends. Maria and Sarah head back to their beach loungers, and decide to relax under the umbrella for a while.

Renting kayaks at the beach

After a refreshing swim and some relaxing time on the beach reading their books, Maria and Sarah want to get out on the water to see the views and be a bit active.

Sarah: Would you be up for renting a kayak or a SUP for an hour? I saw they have both for rent when we got our beach beds at the kiosk. The kayak is just seven euros for an hour.

Maria: Yes, great idea! Let's get kayaks and explore the coastline a bit.

The women go over to the kiosk to rent kayaks.

Maria: Buongiorno. Possiamo noleggiare due kayak per un'ora?

Addetto: Certo. Volete due kayak o un kayak per due persone?

Maria turns to Sarah to get her opinion.

Maria: Do you want us to each have our own kayak, or do you want to share a two person kayak?

Sarah: Let's rent a two person kayak. It's more social, and it's more relaxing to row together.

Maria turns back to the kiosk attendant and tells him that they want a two person kayak. He tells Maria that it costs €7 per hour, and that she can pay when they return.

Maria: Vorrei un kayak per due persone, grazie.

Addetto: Va bene. Costa sette euro all'ora. Può pagare al ritorno.

Maria: Ottimo!

To make the booking the kiosk attendant needs to see some proof of identity, and Maria gives him her passport.

Addetto: Perfetto! Avrei solo bisogno di un documento d'identità per il noleggio.

Maria: Certo, ecco il mio passaporto.

He then tells them that the safety instructions for kayaking are posted near the kiosk, and he asks if they would like life vests. Maria says yes to the life vests, saying she can't wait to go kayaking.

Addetto: Grazie! Le istruzioni per la sicurezza sono affisse vicino al chiosco. Vi darò anche i giubbotti di salvataggio.

Maria: Perfetto, grazie mille! Non vedo l'ora di partire!

The kiosk attendant gives them two sets of kayak oars and points them to where they can find the kayaks.

Addetto: Ecco qui i remi da kayak. Il kayak è là.

The women put on their life vests, take their oars, and take the kayak out on the water. They enjoy an hour of exploring the coastline together. After the hour is up, they put the kayak back where they found it, and return the oars and life vests to the kiosk attendant.

Maria: Ciao. Ecco i remi. Grazie!

Addetto: Grazie!

The kayak trip was fun but a bit tiring, so they head back to their *lettini* to relax in the sun.

Booking a boat tour

The sun is sparkling across the ocean waves and the sea looks particularly inviting this summer day. Many small and big boats are bobbing up and down in the bay, and a ferry is occasionally passing between the different towns and the islands in the distance.

Sarah: It was really fun to go kayaking and see some of the shoreline. The sea is so calm today and the weather is brilliant. Maybe we could see if there's some kind of boat or ferry ride that would let us explore more of the coast line? It could also be fun to go swimming in some of the bays we kayaked past.

Maria: That's a brilliant idea. Let's check if there's a ferry or a boat tour we can book.

They walk over to a small, wooden pier that looks like it might be where ferries and boats dock. At the entrance to the pier there is a large sign that says *traghetto* on it, and a board with a timetable and a map of the *traghetto* routes. There is also an island tour they can buy tickets for that's called *giro delle isole*.

On a board next to the ferry sign there are posters for boat tours. There is a *gita in barca al tramonto*, offering a sunset boat trip. A *gita in barca con pranzo*, a boat trip with lunch, and a *giro privato in barca*, offering a private boat tour.

Sarah: There are a lot of good options here. I'd love to do a half day trip that includes swimming. Do any of them offer that?

Maria: That sounds really nice. Let me have a look.

Maria has a closer look at the posters. She sees a poster saying *Noleggio barche. Mezza giornata o giornata intera*, offering half or full day boat rentals. She also sees a one saying *gita in barca con nuoto*, offering a boat trip with swimming. She points at the last one while translating for Sarah.

Maria: This boat trip includes swimming. See the *con nuoto* here, *nuoto* means swimming. I'll Whatsapp the number on the poster to see if they have space for us this afternoon. For almost all small businesses in Italy, the way to get in touch and book is through Whatsapp, and they usually respond really quickly.

Maria (Whatsapp): Ciao. Avete posto per due persone per la gita con nuoto oggi pomeriggio? Grazie, Maria.

Maria gets a reply on Whatsapp almost immediately.

Venditore (Whatsapp): Ciao. Sì, c'è posto. Ci vediamo al pontile alle 13:30. Pranzate prima, non è incluso.

Maria (Whatsapp): Quanto costa per due persone?

Venditore (Whatsapp): Cinquanta euro in totale. Può pagare dopo con la carta o in contanti.

Maria (Whatsapp): Perfetto, ci vediamo al pontile alle 13:30. Grazie!

Maria puts her phone away with an excited look on her face and turns to Sarah.

Maria: I've booked us into the boat trip with swimming this afternoon. We are to meet them here at the pier at half past one. They recommended we eat lunch first, as lunch is not included.

Sarah: Amazing, I can't wait! Let's go get lunch and our swimsuits.

Lunch at the beach restaurant

At noon Maria and Sarah decide to get lunch at the beach restaurant. It's a casual restaurant with covered outdoor seating on the beach that serves both hot and cold food. They find a free table and sit down. Shortly afterwards, the waitress comes over, hands them menus, and tells them about the daily specials.

Cameriera: Buongiorno. Il primo del giorno è spaghetti al granchio, mentre il pesce del giorno è branzino. Cosa desiderate da bere?

Maria: Dell'acqua frizzante, per favore.

The waiter goes to get their sparkling water, and Maria explains the daily specials to Sarah.

Maria: The first course of the day is spaghetti with crab, and the fish of the day is a *branzino*, which is sea bass and very typical of the region. Let's see what else they have on the menu.

They open the menus and have a look.

Sarah: What's the difference between *primi* and *secondi*?

Maria: An Italian restaurant serves four courses. *Antipasti* is appetizers and starters, and literally means before the meal. It's usually small dishes typical for the region, or cured meats and cheeses. Here by the sea most starters are seafood based. *Primi* is the first course, which is spaghettis and gnocchi. *Secondi* is the second course, typically fish and meat. Then you have *dolci* which are desserts. Coffee is served at the very end, after the dessert as it's believed it closes the stomach.

Sarah: Do we need to eat four courses at every meal?

Maria: No, definitely not! But when you're many people it's nice to share some dishes from each course and enjoy a long dinner. That would be a typical Italian family meal.

Sarah: That sounds like a lovely way of dining. What are you going to have for lunch?

Maria: I was thinking of just having a pasta dish. I'll translate a few of the dishes for you. The *spaghetti ai frutti di mare* is seafood spaghetti with lots of shellfish, scampi and squid - you rarely get fish in it. The *gnocchi con gamberi* is gnocchi with prawns. The *risotto nero alla seppia* is black spaghetti with cuttlefish, and the *penne all'arrabbiata,* which literally means penne the angry way, is penne in a spicy tomato sauce.

Sarah: Thanks for translating. I'll get the *gnocchi con gamberi.*

The waitress returns with their sparkling water, and they place their orders.

Cameriera: Cosa prendete?

Maria: Vorrei gli spaghetti ai frutti di mare.

Sarah: Gnocchi con gamberi, per favore.

A short while later the waitress returns with their food. She puts a big bowl of seafood pasta in front of Maria, with prawns, squid rings, and mussels. Sarah gets a plate with gnocchi and prawns in a pink sauce that looks tomato based. Sarah takes a bite.

Sarah: Yum, this is delicious! The prawns have so much flavour.

They finish their lunches, and in the interest of time decide to skip dessert and go directly for coffee.

Sarah: I would love an iced coffee. How do you get one of those in Italy? *Caffè con ghiaccio*?

Maria: I see you've looked up the word for ice. Iced coffee sounds nice and refreshing, let's do that. You can say *caffè con ghiaccio*, but the more spectacular thing to order is a *caffè shakerato*. It's espresso coffee shaken with ice in a cocktail shaker. *Shakerato* literally means shaken. It's delicious, and usually served in a cocktail glass too.

Sarah: Wow that sounds amazing, let's get that!

The waitress comes over to take their coffee order, and Sarah orders two *shakerati*.

Cameriera: Cosa desiderate?

Sarah: Due caffè shakerati, per favore.

A few minutes later two martini glasses with ice cold coffee appear in front of them, with some shaken coffee foam on top.

Sarah: This looks just like an espresso martini!

Maria: Yes, haha. But no alcohol, just coffee and nothing else.

Sarah: Mmm, it's delicious. I think this is my new favourite coffee now! Why don't we do these at home?

Maria: Great question!

After finishing their coffees, Maria asks the waitress for the bill.

Maria: Il conto, per favore. Voglio pagare con la carta di credito.

Maria pays by credit card, and they go back to their *lettini* to get ready for their *gita in barca con nuoto.*

Boat tour with swimming

It's half past one in the afternoon at the Italian seaside. Sarah and Maria are excitedly waiting at a small, wooden pier in town for their boat tour with swimming. There are a few other people waiting with them as well, so it looks like they will be a group of six in the end. A small rib arrives to pick them up with just enough space for six people to sit comfortably.

Barcaiolo: Ciao! Siete tutti qui per la gita in barca con nuoto?

Passengers: Sì!

Barcaiolo: Mi chiamo Paolo. Sono il vostro capitano per il pomeriggio. Benvenuti a bordo!

Their captain Paolo welcomes them on board the boat, and helps them all into the boat one by one. One of the men looks a little bit nervous on the water, and asks Paolo if he has any life vests he could use.

Uomo: Scusa, hai un giubbotto di salvataggio che posso usare?

Paolo: Certo. Ecco qui. Qualcun altro vuole un giubbotto di salvataggio?

Tutti: No, grazie.

Everyone else mutters that they are happy without a life vest. Paolo starts the boat and sets off along the coast at a leisurely pace. It's a beautiful day for a boat ride. The sun is shining, it's hot, and the sea is calm. There are almost no waves or wind.

Maria: Che bella giornata! Il sole splende, fa caldo e il mare è calmo. Non ci sono quasi onde o vento.

Paolo: Sì, oggi il tempo è perfetto per una gita in barca. Molto tranquillo.

Paolo stops the boat in a quiet bay where a few other boats have also anchored. Some people are swimming from their boats, while others are tanning on deck.

Paolo: Allora. Qui è dove nuoteremo oggi. Mettete il costume da bagno e tuffatevi!

On Paolo's request they all get into their swimming costumes and gleefully jump into the water from the boat. Everyone has fun in the water and swims around for a while, before coming back up onto the boat to rest. One of the men asks Maria if she can pass him his towel.

Uomo: Scusa, puoi passarmi il mio telo mare? È quello blu.

Maria: Sì, certo. Ecco.

Just after Maria hands the man his blue towel, Paolo tells them that they have time for a bit of sunbathing before they head back.

Paolo: Avete tempo per prendere un po' di sole prima di tornare.

They find a space on the boat to bask in the sun and dry up after their swims. One of the men looks to have forgotten his sunscreen and is slowly turning pink. His friend warns him that he's turning pink, and should put on some sunscreen.

Donna: Luigi, stai diventando rosso!

Luigi: Mamma mia! Ho dimenticato la crema solare. Avete della crema solare che posso usare?

It turns out that Luigi has forgotten his sunscreen, which is why he's rapidly turning pink. He asks if anybody on the boat has sunscreen he can borrow. Sarah, who just bought herself a bottle of factor fifty that morning, gives some to Luigi.

Sarah: Puoi prendere un po' della mia, è fattore cinquanta.

Luigi: Grazie mille!

Luigi borrows a bit of Sarah's sunscreen and is very grateful.

After a while, one of the other women on the boat asks if she has time for one last swim before they head back.

Donna: Ho tempo per un'ultima nuotata prima di tornare?

Paolo: Sì, ma fai veloce!

Paolo tells her that she can have a last dip, but she has to be quick. She jumps in and does a last lap around the boat, before coming up to dry off.

Donna: Grazie. Ho finito.

Paolo: Bene. È ora di tornare indietro.

As Paolo tells them it's time to return to shore, they all put their summer clothes back on and settle into the boat. He points the boat back to the port and speeds off. Ten minutes later, they arrive back at the shore, and Paolo helps them from the boat onto the pier.

Maria: Grazie Paolo per la fantastica esperienza!

Paolo: Piacere mio!

Maria and Sarah pay Paolo, and happily go enjoy the rest of their afternoon on the beach.

Dinner by the seaside

Maria and Sarah have had a great but tiring day by the seaside. They spent most of the day on the beach, and also managed to find the time to both rent kayaks and go for an afternoon boat trip with a swim. Now they are ready for dinner. Tonight they are trying the *trattoria* in the piazza that Laura recommended, which offers traditional Italian food typical for the seaside. They have just sat down, and are browsing the menu.

Sarah: I'm starving after all our activities today! Tonight might be the night I want to try all four courses on the menu.

Maria: Haha, I'd be up for that. I'm starving too.

Sarah: Why don't we share a bit of each course? We could get two *antipasti*, one *primi*, one *secondi*, and a *dolce* to share.

Maria: Sounds good. Why don't we try something typical for the seaside? For one of the *antipasti* my vote is for the *cozze ripiene*, which is stuffed mussels in tomato sauce. They are a classic. Which *antipasti* do you want?

Sarah: I'd like to try the *cozze ripiene* too, so let's get that. I've never had stuffed mussels before. How about the *insalata di polpo*?

Maria: Octopus salad as an *antipasti* is usually served in cold slices with cold potatoes. It's a bit of an acquired taste if you ask me. How about we get some *fritto misto*? It's not on the *antipasti* section, it's in *secondi*, but it's a really typical shared starter. It's lightly battered and fried seafood. It's really good. You have to try it while we're down here by the sea.

Sarah: OK, sounds good. What would you like for *primi*? We had pasta earlier today, so how about *risotto allo scoglio*? That's risotto with shellfish right?

Maria: Yes, it's risotto with shellfish and often a bit of tomato. Let's get it. Now for *secondi*, what are you thinking?

Sarah: I'm looking at the *secondi di pesce*. Looks like it's all fish. What is *pesce spada ai ferri*?

Maria: *Pesce* means fish, so it looks like all their second courses are fish based. *Pesce spada* is swordfish, and *ai ferri* means grilled. So it's grilled swordfish.

Sarah: I'm not super keen on swordfish. How about the *filetto di tonno in crosta di pistacchi*, what is that? It sounds like a pistachio crust if I'm not mistaken.

Maria: It's tuna fillet with a pistachio crust. That's probably really nice, and likely served raw in the middle. Let's get that.

When they have decided and closed their menus, the friendly waiter comes over to take their order.

Cameriere: Ditemi, cosa desiderate?

Maria: Come antipasto, le cozze ripiene e il fritto misto. Come primo, il risotto allo scoglio. Come secondo, il filetto di tonno in crosta di pistacchi. Condividiamo tutto.

Maria orders the dishes they discussed to share. The waiter then asks them what wine they would like to have. Maria asks for his recommendations, and he recommends a white Vermentino wine, which is a grape typical of the coastal area.

Cameriere: E da bere? Volete del vino?

Maria: Cosa ci consiglia?

Cameriere: Vi consiglio un Vermentino. È un vino bianco tipico della costa.

Maria: Sembra buono! Prendiamo una bottiglia di Vermentino e una bottiglia d'acqua gassata.

They enjoy a long dinner with many delicious, traditional dishes. The Vermentino wine is fresh and pairs well with their seafood dishes.

The women have just finished their main courses, and are discussing what to get for dessert.

Sarah: I'd love to have a coffee with my dessert.

Maria: In Italy coffee is served after you're done eating, as they believe it closes the stomach, so I'd recommend waiting until after dessert.

Sarah: Ok, let's do that then.

The waiter returns and asks if they'd like dessert.

Cameriere: Desiderate il dolce? Oggi il dolce del giorno è il tiramisù.

Maria: Sì, vorremmo un tiramisù e due cucchiai.

The waiter brings them a tiramisu to share and two spoons. After they finish their delicious dessert, the waiter returns to ask if they'd like coffee.

Cameriere: Desiderate un caffè?

Maria: Si, un caffè macchiato per me.

Sarah: Un caffè normale per me.

The waiter returns with their coffee. He puts an espresso in front of Sarah, and an espresso with a spoon of milk foam on it in front of Sarah. After they have finished their coffee, the waiter surprises them with free limoncello shots.

Cameriere: Limoncello per voi, offerto dalla casa!

Sarah: Grazie mille! Salute!

Maria: Salute!

They drink their complimentary limoncello, pay, and leave the restaurant.

Sarah: I'm so excited to go to Tuscany tomorrow, I can't wait!

The women head back to their hotel to go to bed, eager to continue their adventure in-land to Tuscany tomorrow.

~ CAPITOLO 3 ~

Staying at a Tuscan Agriturismo

Arriving in Tuscany

Today, Sarah and Maria are bidding the seaside farewell and heading in-land to Tuscany. There they will be spending a couple of days at an *agriturismo*. They have found a typical Italian countryside stay on a nice vineyard with a pool. They have decided to take the train to their hotel, as there is a train station a short taxi ride from the agriturismo.

The women find themselves at the train station in the seaside town trying to figure out which train to take, and how to get tickets. Maria walks up to the ticket counter and asks the woman at the counter when the next train to Montelupo is, and to buy two tickets.

Maria: A che ora è il prossimo treno per Montelupo?

Addetta: Tra mezz'ora dalla piattaforma uno. Vuole comprare dei biglietti?

Maria: Sì. Due biglietti per Montelupo, per favore.

Addetto: Certo. Costano venti euro. Contanti o carta?

Maria: Contanti.

Maria gives the woman at the counter a twenty euro bill, and she gives Maria two tickets to Montelupo. Maria takes the tickets and starts making her way to platform one.

Maria: I got us two tickets to Montelupo station. It was twenty euro for both of us. The train leaves in half an hour from platform one. Let's go.

Sarah: Great!

They find their way to platform one and get on the train that stops at Montelupo. They sit down in a square of seats for extra space.

A few stations later, many new passengers come on, and the train becomes more crowded. A woman comes over and asks if the seat that Sarah has her bag in is free, and if she can sit there.

Donna: Scusi, questo posto è libero? Posso sedermi?

Sarah: Sì. Prego.

Sarah moves her bag and luggage around to give the woman space to sit down, and ends up putting her suitcase in the aisle. Not long after, a ticket inspector coming past asks her to move the suitcase onto the overhead shelves so it's not obstructing the aisle.

Controllore: Mi scusi, ma deve mettere la valigia sopra, per favore. Non può bloccare il corridoio.

Sarah: La valigia è troppo pesante per me da sollevare.

Controllore: Nessun problema, la aiuto io.

Since the suitcase is too heavy for Sarah to lift, the ticket inspector helps her lift it onto the overhead shelves, before asking to see their tickets.

Controllore: I biglietti, per favore.

Maria: Ecco i biglietti.

Controllore: Grazie. Buon viaggio!

When they get to Montelupo station, they exit and see some taxis waiting outside. Maria goes up to the first taxi and asks if he can take them to their agriturismo. She shows him the location on google maps on her phone.

Maria: Buongiorno. Può portarci al nostro agriturismo?

Taxi driver: Certo. Dove si trova?

Maria: Ecco, è qui su Google Maps.

Taxi driver: Perfetto. Andiamo.

The taxi driver helps them get the luggage into his car, and drives them to the agriturismo. The taxi drives through winding country roads, past olive groves and vineyards. Tiny stone villages dot the hilltops, surrounded by farmland and forests. On the top of a hill, the driver suddenly makes a left and they drive up a tree-lined country road taking them to a big, Tuscan villa. The taxi stops in front of the villa and the driver helps them with the bags. Maria and Sarah take their bags and go inside to check in.

Checking in at the Agriturismo

Maria and Sarah have just arrived at the agriturismo they are staying at in Tuscany. It's a big Tuscan villa on top of a hill, with sweeping views of the Tuscan countryside. The women head into the villa to check in at reception. There, they are greeted by a friendly, middle-aged woman behind a wooden desk.

Receptionist: Benvenute in Toscana!

Maria: Buongiorno. Ho prenotato una camera per due persone con due letti. Il mio nome è Maria Bianchi.

Receptionist: Buongiorno, signora Bianchi. Posso vedere i documenti d'identità, per favore.

Maria: Certo.

Maria hands their passports to the receptionist, who checks them before handing them the key to room 23.

Receptionist: Ecco qui la sua chiave della camera ventitré. La camera è già pronta.

Maria: Grazie!

Receptionist: La camera si trova al secondo piano. Se desiderate rilassarvi all'aperto, uscendo sulla destra troverete la piscina, con una splendida vista sulla campagna toscana. Se invece amate lo sport, sulla sinistra c'è il campo da tennis.

The receptionist explains that their room is on the 2nd floor. Outside on the right, they can find the swimming pool, which has a beautiful view of the Tuscan countryside. Outside on the left, they can find the tennis court. She goes on to explain that breakfast is in the room on the left side of reception from seven to ten in the morning.

Receptionist: La colazione è dalle sette alle dieci del mattino nella stanza alla sinistra della reception.

The receptionist then hands them a brochure with experiences they can book while at the hotel, including massages and wine tastings.

Receptionist: Ecco una brochure delle esperienze che si possono fare in hotel, tra cui massaggi e degustazioni di vino.

Maria: Grazie.

Finally, she tells them that if they need anything, they shouldn't hesitate to call.

Receptionist: Se avete bisogno di qualcosa, non esiti a chiamarci!

They grab their bags and walk up the stairs to their room on the 2nd floor. Their *camera* is spacious, with stone floors, two *lettini* and a *bagno*. Through the window they have a view of the *piscina* and the rolling Tuscan *colline*.

Sarah: Wow, the view is absolutely stunning! The pool looks really inviting, let's go check it out!

They put their bags down, find their swimwear and head for the *piscina*.

At the *piscina*

The *piscina* at the agriturismo is inviting, with a view over rolling Tuscan *colline*, a selection of fun pool inflatables, and almost no other guests around the pool. Maria and Sarah follow the signs to the *piscina* and put their towels down on two *lettini* with an unobstructed view of the *bella vista*.

Sarah: Look at that *vista*! This truly is a dream *vacanza*.

Maria: *Che vista bellissima*, what a beautiful view! Let's go for a swim in the *piscina*, the water looks so inviting.

The women jump into the *piscina* and swim some casual laps, before stopping to relax and have a chat at one end of the pool. They have the space almost to themselves, with just one Italian couple standing in the water on the other side of the pool. The woman approaches them and asks Sarah if she's using the inflatable flamingo.

Donna: Scusi, sta usando questo fenicottero gonfiabile?

The woman points at the inflatable flamingo next to Sarah.

Sarah: No, non lo uso. Prego.

Sarah indicates to the woman that she can take the inflatable. The woman takes it and floats around the pool on it.

Maria: Well done, your Italian is really improving! You were able to tell the woman you're not using it, and tell her with *prego* that she's welcome to it, in perfect Italian.

Sarah: *Grazie*!

After a bit more swimming Maria and Sarah head back to their *lettini* to relax and read a book in the sun.

Sarah: It's amazing how comfortable the temperature is here. It's a really hot day, but with the slight breeze it's just right.

Maria: Yeah, it's perfect. The trick is to stay on top of a hill. The hilltops get the breeze, so it's comfortable even on a hot summer day. If you're at the bottom of a valley or on the flat it's stiflingly hot, and often flying insects too as the wind doesn't blow them away. So always stay at a Tuscan hotel that's on top of a hill!

Sarah: That's such a great insight. I would never have thought about that!

Maria: I stayed at a hotel on the flats once. I've never been so hot by the pool, nor gotten so many mosquito bites! It's hilltops only for me now.

The women spend the rest of the day relaxing by the pool.

Tuscan lunch

It's lunchtime in Tuscany, and Maria and Sarah have decided to keep it simple and eat a light lunch at the pool bar in the agriturismo.

Sarah: It's so warm today, let's just get something light for lunch like a salad.

Maria: Salads as a main aren't very common in Italy, you usually just get them as a side salad. It looks like we're in luck and the pool bar has a couple of salad options. The *insalata nizzarda* could be good, that's a nicoise salad. Otherwise they have a classic Caesar salad.

Sarah: How about the *insalata caprese*?

Maria: The caprese salad is literally just tomatoes and mozzarella slices. It's not so much a salad as it's meant to be a fresh, shared starter. It is a very classic Italian dish in Tuscany.

Sarah: Ah, in that case I'm going with the Caesar salad.

The waiter comes over to take their order.

Maria: L'insalata nizzarda e l'insalata Caesar, per favore.

At the end of their lunch the waiter asks if they would like any coffees. Maria orders two macchiatos for them.

Cameriere: Volete un caffè?

Maria: Due macchiati, per favore.

Cameriere: Volete il latte freddo o caldo?

Maria: Freddo per me, caldo per lei.

The waiter disappears to make their coffee. Sarah looks puzzled.

Sarah: Why did you order my coffee with cold milk? I want it hot.

Maria Haha, *caldo* very confusingly means hot. *Freddo* means cold.

Sarah: That's so confusing!

A few minutes later the waiter reappears with their coffees. She places the cold macchiato in front of Maria, and the hot macchiato in front of Sarah. She also carries a box of small sugar packets and asks if they would like any sugar with their coffee.

Cameriere: Ecco i vostri caffè macchiati, uno con latte caldo e uno con latte freddo. Desiderate dello zucchero?

Sarah: Sì, grazie.

As Sarah said yes to sugar, the waitress places the box of sugar packets on their table. Maria puts some sugar in her coffee.

Sarah: How is your *freddo* macchiato?

Maria: It's refreshingly cool!

They enjoy their coffees, then pay and leave the restaurant.

Booking experiences

When they checked into the agriturismo, the receptionist gave them a brochure listing the experiences they can book to make their stay more eventful. Sarah and Maria are both having a look through the brochure to see what's on offer. Maria wants to book herself in for a massage, and Sarah wants them to attend a wine tasting of local wines from the agriturismo. They go down to the reception to book their experiences.

Receptionist: Buongiorno, come posso aiutarvi?

Maria: Buongiorno. Vorrei prenotare un massaggio rilassante per me.

Receptionist: Perfetto. Abbiamo disponibilità alle due questo pomeriggio. Le andrebbe bene?

Maria: Grazie! Dove si svolge il massaggio?

Receptionist: Il massaggio è nella nostra spa, vicino alla piscina.

Maria successfully books herself in for a relaxing massage at the spa that afternoon at 2pm. Sarah then asks the receptionist if they can book a wine tasting.

Sarah: Vorrei prenotare la degustazione di vino locale per due persone, per favore.

Receptionist: Certo. Abbiamo disponibilità alle quattro questo pomeriggio. Va bene per voi?

Sarah: Perfetto. Dov'è la degustazione?

Receptionist: La degustazione è nella cantina, sotto il ristorante, a sinistra.

The receptionist finishes booking them in for the wine tasting at 4pm, in the wine cellar below the restaurant.

Getting a massage

Maria is getting a relaxing massage by the masseuse at the agriturismo, and her masseuse only speaks Italian. At the beginning of the session the masseuse introduces herself.

Massaggiatrice: Buongiorno. Mi chiamo Giulia. Sono la tua massaggiatrice per oggi.

Maria: Buongiorno Giulia. Sono Maria. Vorrei un massaggio rilassante, per favore.

Giulia tells Maria that as she massages, Maria should tell her if she wants the massage to be more firm or more gentle.

Giulia: Durante il massaggio, dimmi se lo vuoi più intenso o più delicato.

Maria: Va bene.

Giulia: Per favore, sdraiati sul lettino da massaggio, a pancia in giù.

Giulia asks Maria to lay belly down on the massage table. Maria lies down and they get started. The masseuse gently massages Maria's back and shoulders.

Maria: Più forte, per favore.

Giulia: Certo. Va bene?

Maria: Troppo forte. Un po' più delicato, per favore.

Maria asks Giulia to massage a bit firmer. Giulia goes a bit too firm, and Maria asks her to go a bit lighter.

After a while, the *massaggiatrice* asks Maria to turn around.

Giulia: Girati, per favore.

Maria turns around to face up. The massage goes on for a bit longer before it finishes.

Giulia: Tutto finito.

Maria: Grazie mille per il massaggio rilassante.

Maria is happy to have had a relaxing massage. She feels refreshed, and ready for the wine tasting.

Wine tasting

The wine cellar below the restaurant in the agriturismo is surprisingly large, and looks like it has been there for hundreds of years. Large wooden barrels line both sides of the long room, filling the air with the scent of aged wine and oak. An ancient looking solid wood farmhouse table runs down the centre of the room. It has been set for a wine tasting for two, but could easily fit thirty.

Maria and Sarah are greeted by the man running the wine tasting, who turns out to be the sommelier for the restaurant and also in charge of wine production at the agriturismo.

Sommelier: Benvenuti nella nostra cantina! Mi chiamo Marco. Sono il sommelier.

Maria: Buon pomeriggio. Mi chiamo Maria.

Sara: Ciao. Mi chiamo Sarah.

Sommelier: Sedetevi pure al tavolo.

Marco tells them to take a seat at the table, which has already been set up for their wine tasting. Several wine glasses have been placed in front of each seat, and some bread and oils have also been put out on the table. They sit down, excited to try the first wine.

Sommelier: Oggi degustiamo i prodotti fatti qui nell'agriturismo. Abbiamo tre vini, un olio d'oliva e un aceto balsamico.

The sommelier explains that they will be tasting products created locally at the agriturismo today. There are three house wines, one olive oil, and one balsamic vinegar. He starts by pouring them a glass of yellow white wine.

Sommelier: Primo, degustiamo il vino bianco della casa.

Marco goes on to explain that this is from a Trebbiano Toscano grape, which is one of the most used grapes in Tuscan white wines. It is a dry white wine that has tasting notes of flowers and peaches.

Sommelier: Ha un colore giallo. È fatto con uva Trebbiano Toscano, una delle più usate nei vini bianchi toscani. È un vino bianco secco, con note di fiori e pesche.

They swirl their glasses and smell the wine before tasting. When they take a sip, it feels refreshing. They can just about taste the notes the sommelier mentioned.

Maria: Che buon profumo! Sa di pesche.

Sarah: È delizioso! Sa di fiori.

Next, the sommelier pours them a glass of ruby red wine.

Sommelier: Poi, degustiamo il vino rosso della casa.

The sommelier explains that the red wine is made with a Sangiovese grape, which is very typical of the Tuscany region. It is full-bodied, with tasting notes of cherry, blackberry, and vanilla.

Sommelier: È fatto con uva Sangiovese, molto tipica della Toscana. È un vino corposo, con note di amarena, mora e vaniglia.

They start by swirling and smelling the wine, enjoying the gentle notes of vanilla. Upon tasting the full-bodied wine, they easily notice the main flavours of black cherries and blackberries.

Maria: Squisito! Sa di mora.

Sarah: Ottimo! Sa di amarena.

For the last wine, the sommelier pours them each a small glass of amber wine, which almost looks like liquid gold. He explains that this is Vin Santo, which is typical of the Tuscan region, and made from Trebbiano and Malvasia grapes. The tasting notes are of dried apricots and walnuts.

Sommelier: Infine, degustiamo il Vin Santo della casa. Il Vin Santo è un vino tipico toscano, fatto con uve Trebbiano e Malvasia. Ha un retrogusto di albicocche secche e noci. È un vino dolce da dessert

They take a sip of the sweet wine and enjoy the rich flavours. The wine almost feels like a dessert in itself.

Sarah: È molto dolce! Sa di albicocche.

Maria: Sì, e anche di noci.

Sommelier: Esatto!

He then hands them a dry cantucci biscuit to pair with the Vin Santo.

Sommelier: Prego. Potete mettere i cantucci nel Vin Santo. Li rende morbidi.

They dip the dry cantucci biscuit in the Vin Santo and quickly notice that it softens by soaking up the sweet wine. They try a bite, and the biscuit is now soft and sweet, rather than rock hard.

Sarah: Delizioso!

Maria: È molto dolce. Mi piace.

After the wine, they move onto the olive oil and balsamic vinegar. First, the sommelier asks them to pour a little of the extra virgin olive oil onto their plate and dip their bread into it.

Sommelier: Ora, degustate l'olio d'oliva extra vergine della casa. Potete mettere il pane nell'olio.

They follow the directions from the sommelier, dipping their bread into the olive oil.

Sarah: Molto buono.

The sommelier then asks them to pour a little bit of the balsamic vinegar somewhere else on their plate. They can then dip their bread in it and taste the balsamic vinegar.

Sommelier: Ora, degustate l'aceto balsamico della casa. Potete mettere il pane nell'aceto.

Maria: L'aceto balsamico è molto buono.

Sarah: Sì, mi piace molto.

Finally, the sommelier asks them to mix the olive oil and balsamic vinegar together, and dip their bread in the mix.

Sommelier: Infine, mescolate l'olio e l'aceto, poi mettete il pane dentro.

Sarah: Mi piace tanto!

Maria: Delizioso! Posso avere ancora un po' di pane, per favore?

Sommelier: Certo!

Maria: Grazie mille!

Maria liked the mix of the olive oil and balsamic vinegar on bread so much that she cheekily asks for more bread. The sommelier gives her another basket, and the women enjoy the second basket of bread with the oil and vinegar.

At the end of the tasting, the sommelier hands them a brochure with an overview of the wine and an order form. He tells them that they can order anything they enjoyed tasting.

Sommelier: Potete comprare qualsiasi vino che vi è piaciuto.

The sommelier leaves the room for a bit, giving them some privacy to discuss if they want to buy anything.

Sarah: The olive oil was nice, but the balsamic vinegar really stood out. I would love to bring a small bottle home. I use so little of it that it's going to last a very long time.

Maria: Ok, I'll put a small bottle of balsamic vinegar on the order sheet. I think I'm going to order myself a bottle of the Vin Santo. It was really good as a dessert wine with the cantucci biscuits. That could be a cute and light dessert to offer dinner guests.

Sarah: Add a bottle for me as well, and four bottles of the white. I couldn't get enough of that one. I really hope I can find it in some shop at home later!

The sommelier returns, and asks if there is anything they would like to order. Maria gives him the form, and summarises their order.

Sommelier: Desiderate acquistare qualcosa?

Maria: Sì. Vorremmo quattro bottiglie di vino bianco della casa, due bottiglie di Vin Santo e una piccola bottiglia di aceto balsamico.

Sommelier: Perfetto. Impacchetto il vostro ordine e lo lascio alla reception per il ritiro.

The sommelier takes their order and lets them know he will leave it for them to collect at reception. They finish the wine tasting and head back up to their room.

Dinner in Tuscany

It's dinner time, and Maria and Sarah are having dinner at a local *trattoria* near their agriturismo.

Sarah: Tonight I want to try the local specialities. What's typically Tuscan?

Maria: I'm not sure, let's ask our waiter.

The waiter comes over to take their order.

Cameriere: Buonasera. Cosa desiderate?

Maria: Buonasera. Quali sono le specialità locali toscane?

Cameriere: Come antipasti, la ribollita e i salumi sono piatti tipici toscani. Come primi, le lasagne e gli spaghetti al ragù di cinghiale sono tipici e molto buoni. Come secondo, la bistecca alla fiorentina è una specialità.

Sarah: Che cos'è la ribollita?

Cameriere: La ribollita è una zuppa tipica toscana, preparata con pane raffermo, fagioli cannellini, cavolo nero e verdure.

Maria asks the waiter which dishes he recommends.

Maria: Cosa ci consiglia?

Cameriere: Consiglio la ribollita come antipasto e, come secondo, la bistecca alla fiorentina, che è il nostro piatto più famoso.

The waiter recommends the ribollita soup as a starter, and the famous bistecca alla fiorentina as a main. Maria and Sarah briefly discuss what they want before placing their order.

Maria: I'd like to start with the ribollita soup, but I want to save the bistecca fiorentina for when we're actually in Florence in a few days, so I think I'll have the spaghetti with wild boar ragu. What are you thinking?

Sarah: Yeah I agree. I'll also start with the ribollita, and then have the lasagna.

They give their order to the waiter.

Maria: Come antipasto, vorrei la ribollita. Poi, gli spaghetti al ragù di cinghiale.

Sarah: Anch'io vorrei la ribollita come antipasto. Come primo, vorrei la lasagna, per favore.

Cameriere: Cosa desiderate da bere? Vi consiglio il vino rosso della casa. È un Sangiovese corposo.

Maria: Perfetto, lo prendiamo.

The waiter recommends that they pair their meal with the house red, which is a full-bodied Sangiovese. Maria orders a bottle.

They enjoy their hearty tuscan meal outdoors, listening to the chatter of the other guests and the crickets in the olive trees. The temperature is balmy, and it's a beautiful, starry night.

~ CAPITOLO 4 ~

Exploring Tuscany

Cycling in the countryside

It's a beautiful, sunny day and Maria and Sarah have decided to borrow *biciclette* from their agriturismo to explore the Tuscan countryside.

Sarah: Let's follow the signs to the nearby town and explore it!

On their way to visit the local town for some sightseeing, they set off down winding country lanes, following the signs for the *paese* and *strada del vino*. As they cycle, they mostly have the roads to themselves as they pass by expansive vineyards and olive groves.

After taking a left turn down a country road, they suddenly find themselves at the end of the road, standing in the courtyard of a local vineyard. A sign by the entrance said *Cantina delle Colline*, or winery of the hills. There is a small sign in the courtyard that says *visite e degustazioni disponibili*, indicating that tours and tastings are available. This is not the local town they were aiming to get to.

Looking for someone to give them directions, they spot an old grandpa walking across the courtyard. Maria waves him down to ask for help. She explains that they are lost, and that they were trying to bike to the local town, but took a wrong turn.

Maria: Buongiorno! Ci può aiutare?

Nonno: Benvenuti nella nostra piccola cantina! Come posso aiutarvi?

Maria: Ci siamo perse. Vogliamo arrivare al paese in bici, ma abbiamo sbagliato strada.

Nonno: Nessun problema. Visto che siete qui, degustate il nostro vino!

Maria: Buona idea!

Nonno: Lasciate le biciclette e facciamo un giro della cantina.

The old man waves for them to follow him as he walks out of the courtyard.

Maria quickly parks her bicycle to the side of the courtyard. At the same time she briefly explains what happened to Sarah, who looks puzzled as to why Maria is leaving her bike behind and is now following the old man.

Maria: Since we're already here, the grandpa has invited us to try their wine and have a tour of the vineyard.

Sarah: We get to experience an authentic Tuscan winery? This is amazing, let's go!

The grandpa starts by taking them to see his vineyard. He turns out to be the owner, and proudly tells them how they only grow top quality Sangiovese grapes.

Nonno: Coltiviamo solo uva Sangiovese di alta qualità in questa cantina.

As they walk through the grape vines, he tells them about the grapes and the vineyard as Maria and Sarah marvel at its size and beauty.

Sarah: La sua cantina è bellissima!

Maria: Sì, davvero meravigliosa!

Nonno: Grazie. È della nostra famiglia da tanto tempo.

Maria: E cosa fate con l'uva?

Nonno: Facciamo il vino. Venite, vi porto a vedere le macchine.

After their walk through the grape vines, they get a tour of the winery machines.

Sarah: Che macchine grandi!

Maria: E poi, cosa fate?

Nonno: Dopo, mettiamo il vino nelle botti. Venite, andiamo in cantina.

They go down to the wine cellar. As they enter, they see a long room with giant oak barrels. Further into the cellar, as they enter rooms off to the side, the walls are lined with racks holding rows upon rows of wine bottles. Some are clearly new, others are ancient looking and covered in dust.

Nonno: Benvenute in cantina! Questo è il nostro vino.

Maria: Che cantina enorme, e che botti grandi!

Sarah: Quante bottiglie! Possiamo assaggiare il vino?

Nonno: Certo! Vi faccio assaggiare un po' di vino.

The grandpa stops between some large wine barrels in oak. He finds a couple of wine glasses and place them on an old, upright barrel that has been repurposed as a table.

Nonno: Prima, assaggiate questo vino bianco. È leggero e fresco, con un gusto rinfrescante di agrumi e mele.

He pours them both a small glass of white wine to taste. It's light and fresh, with a refreshing taste of citrus and apple.

Maria: Questo vino bianco è fresco. Sa di agrumi.

When they have finished tasting it, he pours them each a glass of red wine.

Nonno: Ora, degustate questo vino rosso. È di corpo medio e con note intense di amarena.

They taste the ruby red wine he just poured them. It is medium bodied with notes of black cherries.

Maria: Mi piace molto questo vino rosso. Sa di amarene. Posso comprare una bottiglia?

Nonno: Certo!

After they have had a tour of the small vineyard, tried some of the wines, and bought a bottle to bring back with them, it's time to actually find the local town. They thank the grandpa for the tour of the vineyard and the wine tasting.

Maria: Grazie per il giro e la degustazione.

Nonno: Di niente! Sono contento che vi sia piaciuto.

Then they get back onto their bikes, and the grandpa gives them directions to the town.

Nonno: Andate dritto, poi prendete la prima a sinistra. Dopo, all'incrocio girate a destra. Il paese è lì. Buon viaggio!

Sarah: Grazie mille!

Maria: Arrivederci!

Maria and Sarah follow the grandpa's directions to town. They go straight, then take the first left, then a bit later they turn right and end up in the local town.

Visiting the local Tuscan town

Mara and Sarah have just arrived in the local town, near the Tuscan agriturismo they are staying at. It's nestled on top of a hill, with tightly packed stone houses, narrow pedestrian streets, and several prominent church spires.

Sarah: Wow, the town is beautiful. I love how ancient it looks. It's all stone and winding streets. Let's go explore!

Maria: Yes, let's!

Leaving their bicycles at the town gate, they start exploring by walking through the old stone archway leading into the town. They follow the pedestrian path as it winds up the hill. On either side are small shops selling their wares. By the gate is a gelateria offering a large selection of colourful gelato. There are various shops selling olive oils, hand painted ceramics, and vibrant summer clothes.

At the top of the street they enter into an open piazza with a partial view of the surrounding countryside, an old church, and a couple of outdoor restaurants. There are benches to rest on below some large trees, where people can sit and enjoy the view in the shade. Off to one side, some pensioners are playing boule on a small, sandy pitch.

Sarah: This might be the most idyllic town I've ever visited.

Maria: It's beautiful.

At the coffee bar

While exploring a local Tuscan town, Maria and Sarah spot a small coffee bar. Outside on the street are a few tables with patrons enjoying their coffees. Inside, it only has space for a bar counter that stretches the length of the little shop, with a large coffee machine on top.

Sarah: I would love a coffee actually. Let's grab one of the tables outdoors with a view of people walking past.

Maria: Sounds good.

They find a free table outdoors and the waitress comes over to take their order.

Cameriera: Buongiorno. Cosa desiderate?

Sarah: Vorrei un caffelatte. Che tipo di latte avete?

The waitress looks a bit confused at the question.

Cameriera: Abbiamo latte freddo o caldo.

Sarah looks speechless, and Maria bursts out laughing.

Sarah: Allora un caffelatte con latte caldo, per favore.

Maria: Per me, un caffè macchiato con latte freddo, per favore.

Cameriera: Va bene.

The waitress heads back into the bar with their orders.

Sarah: I don't think that was a weird question. I just really wanted an oat latte.

Maria: In Italy they really only do normal cow's milk, so you won't really find the alternative milk options here; like almond, oat, soy, and so on. Especially not in a tiny, Tuscan town!

Maria bursts out laughing again.

Not long after, the waitress returns with their coffees.

Cameriera: Ecco il caffelatte con latte caldo.

Sarah: Grazie.

Cameriera: Ecco il caffè e il latte freddo.

Sarah: Grazie.

She places a caffè latte with hot milk in front of Sarah, and a cup of espresso in front of Maria with a tiny jug of cold milk next to it. Maria pours some of the cold milk into her coffee.

Sarah: Why don't they just serve you your macchiato with cold milk, why do they give you a jug of milk on the side?

Maria: It's quite common, so you can get the coffee exactly how you want. Many places do it when you order an americano as well. You get a large cup with a shot of espresso in it, and a jug of warm water on the side.

Sarah: The coffee is delicious at least, even if they didn't have alternative milks.

Maria: Yes, my macchiato is very good.

They finish their coffees, pay, and continue exploring the ancient town.

Shopping at a local market

While exploring their local Tuscan town, Maria and Sarah walk down a street that suddenly opens up into a large piazza with market stalls all around the edges. The stalls in the piazza mainly sell fresh produce; like *formaggi*, *salumi*, *frutta*, *pesce*, *fiori*, and *pane*.

Sarah: It's a local market! Let's go check it out.

Sarah walks straight over to the closest stall, which is a *salumeria*. In front of the stall are piles of salami and other dried meats. The counter and the wall behind the vendor are lined with hams in all shapes and sizes.

Sarah: The selection is amazing! Let's get something to bring back to the hotel with us.

Maria: Sounds good. What would you like?

Sarah: The *prosciutto cotto* looks really good, as does the *mortadella* with the pistacchio pieces.

Maria: They are probably delicious, but unless you're planning to eat them right now, there is no way cooked hams will keep all the way back to the hotel in this heat. If it is outside on a hot summer day for several hours, *prosciutto crudo, bresaola* or *salame* are the only safe choices really.

Sarah: Fair point. Let's get a few hundred grams of the crudo to take with us, but I want to try some mortadella too. I can just buy some bread from the baker next-door to eat it with.

Maria: OK, sounds like a plan.

Maria grabs a *salame* from the table and places it on the counter while greeting the vendor.

Maria: Buongiorno.

Venditore: Buongiorno. Cosa desidera?

Maria: Vorrei questo salame e un etto di mortadella con il pistacchio, per favore.

Venditore: Va bene.

The vendor cuts her a hundred grams of mortadella with pistacchio pieces on his large meat slicer. They come out as perfectly cut, paper thin slices that he places flat in a paper pack and weighs, before handing it to her.

Venditore: Ecco la mortadella. Le serve qualcos'altro?

Maria: Sì, vorrei anche mezzo chilo di prosciutto crudo di Parma.

Venditore: Va bene.

The vendor puts the mortadella back on the shelf and gets the large parma ham down into the slicer. He cuts half a kilo of parma ham, which he carefully places in another flat paper pack with thin films of plastic between each layer of ham, to prevent them from sticking together. He then hands the large pack of cured ham to Maria.

Venditore: Ecco il prosciutto crudo. Qualcos'altro?

Maria: No, basta così.

Venditore: In totale sono venti euro.

Maria: Ecco a lei. Grazie mille!

Venditore: Buona giornata!

The vendor gives Maria the bag with her products and wishes her a good day.

Next to the *salumeria* stall is a *formaggeria* stall that sells cheese. In front of the *formaggeria* there are several tables stacked high with round cheeses. A large selection of soft and hard cheeses are being kept cool inside the counter. They recognise some familiar cheese types like *mozzarella, burrata, taleggio* and *pecorino*.

Sarah: I think there are more cheeses here than I've seen in my entire life leading up to this point.

Maria: Haha, let's get something that won't go bad in the heat. Not something from the chilled section.

Sarah grabs one of the round cheeses from the table next to her.

Sarah: I don't know what this one is, but I'd like to try it.

Sarah sets the cheese on the counter and greets the vendor.

Sarah: Buongiorno. Vorrei questo formaggio, per favore.

Venditore: Buongiorno. Va bene. Ti serve qualcos'altro?

Sarah: Sì, un pezzo di Parmigiano Reggiano.

Venditore: Questo pezzo è da quattro etti. Va bene?

The vendor picks up a piece of parmesan that weighs 400 grams and asks if the size is OK. Sarah asks if he has something smaller.

Sarah: No, ha un pezzo più piccolo?

Venditore: Ho questo. Pesa due etti.

Sarah: Va bene, lo prendo.

Venditore: Perfetto. Qualcos'altro?

Sarah: No, basta così. Grazie.

Sarah pays for the cheese, and sets her sight on the *panetteria* bread stall next to it. She wants to get some bread to have with the mortadella they just bought. The stall has a mix of fresh loaves of bread, focaccia, pastries, and cakes. Sarah goes up to the vendor to order a piece of plain focaccia to have with her mortadella.

Sarah: Buongiorno.

Venditore: Buongiorno. Cosa desidera?

Sarah: Vorrei questo pezzo di focaccia, per favore.

Sarah points at a piece of focaccia and asks the vendor if she can have it. The vendor points back at the piece to confirm it's the right one.

Venditore: Questo?

Sarah: Sì.

The vendor puts the focaccia piece in a paper bag and hands it to Sarah. Sarah pays the vendor and takes her focaccia.

In the center of the piazza are some benches next to a large fountain with sculptures on it. They sit down on one of the benches to enjoy their newly purchased foods. Sarah puts some mortadella on the focaccia. She hands half to Maria, and takes a big bite of her own.

Sarah: This is divine!

Maria: *Delizioso!*

Sarah: I think it's made me more hungry than anything. Maybe we should go find a place to have actual lunch, so we have energy to bike back to the agriturismo?

Maria: Good idea. Let's find a restaurant.

They get up from the benches and head back towards the central piazza in search of a lunch restaurant.

Local town lunch

Heading back into the town's open piazza, Maria and Sarah find a restaurant with a terrace out back that has a view of the Tuscan countryside. They ask if it's possible to get a table outside.

Maria: Buongiorno. Avete un tavolo fuori per due?

Cameriere: Avete una prenotazione?

Maria: No.

Cameriere: Va bene, venite con me.

They are in luck, and manage to get a table for two on the terrace. Soon after, the waiter comes over with menus.

Maria: I think I'll have the *vitello*. I rarely see veal on the menu back home. Looking at the *contorni*, I'll have an *insalata mista* and some *verdure grigliate* on the side. You're welcome to have some of my mixed salad and grilled vegetables.

Sarah: That sounds delicious. Do you know what *cotoletta milanese* is?

Maria: Yes, it's a breaded veal cutlet, usually served with a small side of *spaghetti al pomodoro*, so tomato pasta.

Sarah: I'm definitely having that.

While they decide, the waiter comes to take their drinks orders.

Cameriere: Cosa desiderate da bere?

Maria: Dell'acqua gassata, per favore.

They close their menus, and the waiter takes their order.

Cameriere: Siete pronte per ordinare?

Maria: Sì. Vorrei il vitello con le verdure grigliate e un'insalata mista.

Sarah: Vorrei la cotoletta alla milanese con gli spaghetti al pomodoro, per favore.

Cameriere: Va bene.

While waiting for their food, they enjoy the view of the Tuscan countryside. Rolling hills stretch on for as far as the eye can see. The hillsides are a mix of vineyards and olive groves. Tuscan villas and tiny towns dot the hilltops. Narrow roads snake between the hills, with the odd car or cycling pair making their way from one place to another.

When the food finally arrives, it's a masterpiece of Italian cooking. The waiter places a thin and perfectly cooked veal cutlet in front of Maria, with a plate of chargrilled vegetables on one side, and a small bowl of freshly mixed green salad on the other. Sarah's plate is oval and the size of two normal ones, with a large and thin breaded veal cutlet taking up the full plate. A slice of lemon has been left on one side of the plate. The waiter also gives Sarah a small bowl of spaghetti with tomato sauce on the side.

Sarah: Wow, this is the biggest breaded cutlet I've ever seen. And it's so thin!

The waiter holds up a parmesan cheese and asks Sarah if she would like some parmesan on her food.

Cameriere: Vuoi un po' di parmigiano?

Sarah: Sì, grazie.

The waiter puts a bit of parmesan cheese on Sarah's breaded cutlet and a bit on the tomato pasta. He then asks if she'd like more, and she says it's enough.

Cameriere: Vuoi ancora parmigiano?

Sarah: Basta così.

The waiter disappears inside with the parmesan, and Sarah takes a bite of her food.

Sarah: The *cotoletta milanese* tastes delicious, especially paired with the tomato pasta. Who would have thought this was two dishes to mix?

Maria: My *vitello* is fantastic as well. Thin and juicy. Feel free to have some of my *verdure grigliate* and *insalata mista*.

Sarah: Thanks. Do feel free to have some of my *spaghetti al pomodoro*.

The waiter comes back to ask if everything is to their liking.

Cameriere: Tutto bene?

Maria: Delizioso!

Sarah: Molto bene!

They enjoy their Tuscan lunch. Afterwards, they feel energised to bike back towards their agriturismo.

Visiting an olive oil mill

Cycling back from the *paese* to their agriturismo, Sarah and Maria bike past an olive grove and spot a sign saying *frantoio oleario* pointing the way to an olive oil mill. They decide to visit to see if they can taste the local oil. They park their bikes in the courtyard near the sign saying *visite e degustazioni*, that invites people in to visit and taste the olive oil, and enter the main building.

Addetto: Buongiorno!

Maria: Buongiorno! È possibile fare una degustazione di olio d'oliva?

Commesso: Certo! Venite con me.

The welcoming shop assistant indicates that they should follow him. He takes them through to the next room, which is lined with large bottles of olive oil.

They are shown to a counter, and the shop assistant brings out a plate of bread to try the oil with. He explains that they will be trying the shop's own olive oil, which is made from locally grown olives.

Commesso: Allora. Questo è il nostro olio d'oliva. È fatto con olive locali. Provatelo con il pane.

The *commesso* pours some *olio d'oliva* into small bowls for Sarah and Maria to dip the *pane* into.

Maria: Mmm, che buono! Ha un sapore fruttato.

Sarah: Sì, è molto buono!

Commesso: È olio extra vergine di alta qualità. Potete comprare una bottiglia se vi piace.

Maria turns to Sarah.

Maria: He's saying we can buy a bottle of olive oil if we like. What do you think?

Sarah: The olive oil is delicious! Let's get two small bottles, so we each can take one home with us in our luggage.

Maria turns back to the shop assistant.

Maria: Vorremmo comprare due piccole bottiglie, per favore.

Addetto: Perfetto! Vi prendo due piccole bottiglie.

The addetto goes to get two small bottles of olive oil for them, which they pay for by card.

Happy with their excursion, they get their bikes and cycle back to their agriturismo.

Local town festival

Sarah and Maria have just come back from their bike ride in the Tuscan countryside. They are handing their bikes back at the reception when the receptionist tells them about a medieval summer festival happening at the local town tonight, and asks if they want space on the minibuss they've arranged to get there.

Receptionist: Stasera c'è una festa medievale nel paese. È una bella festa che si fa ogni anno. Volete venire con il nostro minibus?

Maria: Sì! A che ora parte il minibus?

Receptionist: Il minibus parte alle sei e ritorna alle undici.

Maria turns to Sarah to tell her about the festival.

Maria: The receptionist just told me that there's an annual medieval festival at the local town tonight. They've arranged a minibus that leaves from here at six pm and returns at eleven pm. I said yes to going. This is going to be amazing. Italian summer festivals are the best. The medieval ones are usually really fun with costumes, fire jugglers, and stalls selling local crafts.

Sarah: That sounds like a cultural experience we can't miss! *Andiamo*!

At six in the evening the minibuss takes them through winding country roads to the local *paese*, where the *festa medievale* is already underway. The narrow streets are packed with revelers. There is music, stalls selling local crafts, and entertainment on every corner. They walk through the streets, enjoying the sights and sounds of the festival. The smell of roasted nuts and freshly made pizza fills the air. Sarah walks over to one of the stalls selling food.

Sarah: I'm getting a bit hungry from all the delicious food smells wafting about. Let's get something small to eat.

Maria: The piadinas from this stall look tasty. They're convenient to eat on the go, as they are just fillings in a folded flatbread.

Maria places an order for *due piadine* with ham and cheese from the woman at the food stall.

Maria: Buonasera. Vorrei due piadine con prosciutto e formaggio, per favore.

Venditrice: Buonasera. Ecco qui le piadine. In totale sono otto euro.

Maria: Ecco otto euro. Grazie!

Venditrice: Prego. Buona serata!

They take their *piadine* from the stall vendor and enjoy them while walking through the bustling town.

As the night goes on, the crowds thicken and the music gets louder. There are fire jugglers, people dancing in medieval costumes, and children playing with foam swords in the streets. The festival is a big hit with everyone, both young and old.

Sarah stops in front of a stall selling leather bags. The stall owner greets her, and tells her how all the bags are hand made from real leather.

Venditore: Buonasera! Tutte le borse sono fatte a mano con vera pelle. C'è qualcosa che ti piace?

Maria: Mi interessa quella borsa nera. Quanto costa?

Venditore: Questa borsa costa trenta euro.

Maria: Va bene, la prendo. Posso pagare con la carta?

Venditore: No, solo in contanti.

Maria: Ecco cinquanta euro.

Venditore: Ecco venti euro di resto. Buona serata!

Maria pays for the bag with cash and happily takes her new black handbag. They continue browsing the stalls.

At eleven o'clock at night Maria and Sarah take the minibus back to the hotel. They are tired, but happy to have taken part in such a fun *festa medievale*.

Checking out

After two eventful days in Tuscany, it's time to head to the next destination - Florence. Maria and Sarah have taken their luggage down to the reception at the agriturismo and are checking out.

Receptionist: Buongiorno.

Maria: Buongiorno. Vorrei fare il check-out, per favore.

Receptionist: Qual è il numero della sua camera?

Maria: La camera numero ventitré.

Receptionist: Ha preso qualcosa dal minibar?

Maria: Sì. Una bottiglia d'acqua naturale e un sacchetto di arachidi salate.

Receptionist: Allora. In totale sono trecentocinquantasei euro da pagare. Ecco il POS.

They successfully check out and pay €356 for their room, including the bottle of water and the small bag of salted peanuts they ate from the mini bar.

Receptionist: Avete bisogno di un taxi per la stazione?

Maria: Sì, grazie.

The receptionist calls them a taxi to the station, and tells them it will arrive in twenty minutes.

Receptionist: Il taxi arriva tra venti minuti.

Maria: Grazie.

They go outside and enjoy the last of the sunny Tuscan countryside. Twenty minutes later, the taxi arrives.

Taxi Driver: Buongiorno. Lei si chiama Maria?

Maria: Sì. Ho prenotato un taxi per la stazione.

Taxi Driver: Perfetto. Posso aiutarvi con le valigie?

Maria: Sì, grazie. Ecco la mia valigia.

Sarah: Ciao. Ecco anche la mia valigia.

After having confirmed that he's picking up the right people, the taxi driver helps them put their bags in the trunk and takes them to the station. There, they will take the train to their next stop — Florence.

~ CAPITOLO 5 ~

Visiting Florence

Arriving in Florence

It's ten o'clock in the morning when Maria and Sarah arrive in Florence. The sun is already high, and it's going to be a hot day. The streets are bustling with both locals and tourists going about their day. On the way to their hotel, they admire the architecture of the ancient city. The taxi takes them from the train station through winding, narrow streets that were clearly created long before cars were invented. Paved roads frequently give way to cobblestones, and pedestrians walk both in the roads and on narrow pavements hugging the low buildings. Each stone building is a small artwork in itself, meticulously decorated with ornate details.

The taxi eventually pulls up to a nondescript building with a sign outside indicating that they have arrived at the right hotel, and the driver helps them with their bags before racing down the street. They take their luggage and carry it up the few steps leading into the hotel reception. Inside, they are greeted by a smiling receptionist in a white shirt and burgundy blazer, who they approach to check in.

Receptionist: Benvenute a Firenze! Posso aiutarvi?

Maria: Buongiorno. Ho una prenotazione a nome di Maria Bianchi.

Receptionist: Il check-in è alle tre. Un momento... Controllo se la vostra camera è pronta.

They try to check in, but the receptionist informs them that check in isn't until 3pm. She still makes an effort to check if their room happens to be ready early, but unfortunately it's not. They are luckily able to leave their bags with the receptionist while they go explore the city.

Receptionist: Mi dispiace, la vostra camera non è ancora pronta.

Sarah: Capisco. Possiamo lasciare i bagagli qui?

Receptionist: Certo! Potete lasciare i bagagli qui con me.

Feeling hungry, Maria asks if there are any good places to get breakfast nearby. The receptionist recommends a bar down the street on the right, just a two minute walk away.

Maria: Grazie! C'è un bar vicino per fare colazione?

Receptionist: Sì, c'è un bar a destra, a due minuti a piedi. Fanno un'ottima colazione!

Having been recommended a place to eat breakfast, Maria then asks how they can get to the main piazza in Florence, *Piazza del Duomo*, where the famous Florence cathedral is. The receptionist tells them that it's a short ten minute walk from the hotel. They just take a right, walk past the bar, then take a left and walk straight until they arrive at the piazza.

Maria: Come arriviamo alla Piazza del Duomo?

Receptionist: Uscite e andate a destra. La piazza è a dieci minuti a piedi. Dopo il bar, girate a sinistra. Poi andate sempre dritto e siete arrivate a Piazza del Duomo.

Maria: Grazie. A dopo.

Receptionist: Vi aspetto alle tre.

They leave their bags with the receptionist and exit the hotel. After taking a right out the door and walking for two minutes, they find the bar the receptionist recommended. It is popular, with many patrons enjoying coffee and a pastry. They have a quick coffee and pastry at the bar, before heading to the *Piazza del Duomo* to see the main sights, including the *Duomo di Firenze*.

Sightseeing in Florence

It's their first and only day in Florence, so Maria and Sarah are eager to make the most of the day and see the main sights. The famous Florence *duomo* is a short walk from their hotel, so they start by heading there. They can see the top of the large *duomo* that is sticking up above the rooftops, and growing ever larger as they draw closer to the historic centre of Florence.

Suddenly, the street they are on opens up into a large piazza with a street sign that says *Piazza del Duomo*. Towering above the other buildings in the piazza, and taking up most of the space, is the famous cathedral *Duomo di Firenze*.

Maria: Welcome to the heart of Florence!

Sarah: Wow, it's stunning! I've never seen a city centre as beautiful.

Maria: Yes, this square is a work of art. On the left you can see the unmissable *Duomo di Firenze*. If we walk straight through the piazza and down towards the river, we will find the world famous Uffizi gallery, with an unrivalled collection of Italian Renaissance art.

Sarah: What does *duomo* mean anyway?

Maria: *Duomo* is used to refer to the major church in a city, which typically is a cathedral, but not always.

Sarah: Let's go inside.

They cross the piazza and head towards the entrance of the duomo. As they get closer, they notice a giant line snaking its way from the entrance and across part of the piazza.

Sarah: Oh no, is that the line to get in?

Maria: Looks like it. I guess we should have gotten here really early to avoid queueing. This is probably going to take a couple of hours and we're only here today. Do you want to join the queue, or should we just admire it from the outside?

Sarah: Let's just admire it from the outside.

They leave the queue, and go for a slow walk around the duomo to take it all in. When they get to the other side of the duomo, they happen to bump into an Italian tour group with a guide who is explaining some of the history of the piazza and the duomo.

Guida: Questo è il Duomo di Firenze, la Cattedrale di Santa Maria del Fiore. L'esterno è di marmo verde, rosa e bianco. È molto famoso per la sua grande cupola di Brunelleschi. La costruzione inizia nel 1296 e finisce nel 1436.

The guide makes a sweeping gesture towards the Duomo while explaining that the outside is made of green, pink and white marble. He goes on to explain that it is very famous for its large dome, created by the famous Italian engineer Brunelleschi. The construction of the cathedral started in 1296, and finished in 1436.

Guida: La nostra prossima tappa è una riproduzione della statua del David fuori da Palazzo Vecchio, poi vedremo opere d'arte dentro la Galleria degli Uffizi. Andiamo!

After stopping to listen to the Italian tour group for a bit, they cheekily follow along as the guide takes his group down the road in the direction of the river. Their first stop is to see the reproduction of Michelangelo's famous David statue outside the Palazzo Vecchio, then the tour group will go look at the art inside the Uffizi Gallery.

Guida: Ecco la riproduzione della statua del David, scolpita da Michelangelo tra il 1501 e il 1504. È alta più di cinque metri. Il David è un simbolo di forza e bellezza per Firenze. Guardate i dettagli: i muscoli, le mani, l'espressione del viso... sembra vivo! Voglio degli addominali così!

Standing in front of Michelangelo's David, the guide tells them that it was sculpted between 1501 and 1504 and is over five metres tall. The statue is a symbol of the beauty and strength of Florence. The guide then draws their attention to the finer details of the statue that make it look so lifelike. The finely sculpted muscles, hands, and the expression on its face. He then points to the middle of the statue, says he wants abs like that, and loudly laughs at his own joke.

After admiring the remarkably lifelike statue of David for a while, the guide takes his group the short walk down the street to the Uffizi gallery. He stops outside and briefly explains its history.

Guida: Questa è la Galleria degli Uffizi. È uno dei musei più importanti d'Italia e uno dei più visitati. È anche uno dei più grandi e famosi al mondo! Qui potete vedere opere d'arte del Rinascimento. Alcune opere famose sono di artisti come Botticelli, Leonardo da Vinci e Raffaello.

The guide explains that the world-famous Uffizi Gallery is one of the most important and most visited museums in Italy. Here, they can see masterworks from the renaissance period, and famous works by artists like Botticelli, Leonardo da Vinci and Raphael.

The Italian tour group has tickets to the Uffizi Gallery, and skips the long line to go straight inside, leaving Maria and Sarah behind outside.

Maria: That was a really good crash course in Florentine history. We were so lucky to bump into that group.

Sarah: Yes, what an efficient way to get the highlights in!

Maria: Do you want to go to the Uffizi gallery? It looks like it also has quite a long queue, and we forgot to pre-order tickets online to skip the queue.

Sarah: Let's skip it, given we have so many things we want to do today. Between the Uffizi gallery and the Duomo we now have two reasons to come back to Florence! And we will plan in advance next time.

Maria: Sounds good. Where to next?

Sarah: Let's check out the Piazzale Michelangelo. I've heard it has the best panoramic view of Florence. It's across the river somewhere.

They quickly check the general directions on their phone, and start heading towards the hill that the Piazzale Michelangelo is on.

Asking for directions in Florence

It's a beautiful day in Florence without a single cloud in the sky, making it the perfect day to get a panoramic picture of the city. Sarah discovered online that they can get amazing panoramic pictures from the Piazzale Michelangelo on the hill above the city. Walking from the duomo, they just have to cross the river and head up a hill. At least those are the directions she's seen. It doesn't take long before they feel lost, and Maria asks a passing woman for directions.

Maria: Scusi, sa come si arriva al Piazzale Michelangelo?

Donna: Ciao. Sì, devi attraversare il ponte, poi prendi a sinistra e sali la collina.

Maria: Grazie!

The woman tells them to walk straight across the bridge, then take a left and go up the hill. Maria thanks her, and they follow her directions across the bridge. After taking a left and walking along the river for a while, they see multiple streets going up the hill and are not sure which one to take, so they ask a passing man for directions.

Maria: Scusi, può dirmi come arrivare al Piazzale Michelangelo?

Uomo: Attraversa la strada, poi prendi la seconda via a sinistra. Quando arrivi a un incrocio con il cartello Giardino delle Rose, prendi l'altra strada.

Maria: Grazie!

Uomo: Sulla via del ritorno, dovresti visitare il Giardino delle Rose. I fiori sono bellissimi e la vista è meravigliosa.

The man tells them to cross the street and take the second road to the left. When they reach a fork in the road with a sign to the rose gardens, they need to take the other road. He recommends that they visit the rose garden on the way back down again, as the flowers are beautiful and the view is marvellous.

Maria and Sarah follow the directions the man gave them. They make it past the fork in the road, and remember to not follow the sign to the rose garden. They are finally walking up the hill, but after walking and walking for a while they want to make sure they're actually on the right road, so Maria asks a woman coming past.

Maria: Scusi, questa strada porta al Piazzale Michelangelo?

Donna: Sì, continua a seguire la strada dritto su per la collina. Devi solo girare a destra quando sei quasi in cima. C'è un cartello.

Maria: Grazie mille!

They continue walking uphill in the baking heat, following the woman's directions to go straight and only turn right when they are almost at the top. Finally, they see the sign for Piazzale Michelangelo and reach their destination. The view from the *piazzale* is absolutely stunning, offering a panoramic view over the whole city of Florence. The duomo sticks up above the rest of the buildings, creating a nice point of interest in the view.

At the *piazzale* there are lots of other people also taking pictures of the view. Maria and Sarah manage to get to the edge and take some nice photos and selfies. A woman seeing that they are taking selfies ask if they'd like her to take a photo of them.

Donna: Scusi, volete una foto con la bella vista panoramica?

Maria: Sì, grazie!

Maria and Sarah line up in front of the view, and the woman takes a couple of nice photos of them. She then asks if they can take a photo of her.

Donna: Potete fare una foto anche a me?

Maria: Certo!

Maria takes a few photos of the woman, before wishing her a good day.

Maria: Ecco qui. Buona giornata!

Donna: Buona giornata!

After working so hard to find and get up to the *piazzale*, Maria and Sarah spend a bit more time enjoying the view before heading back down. They remember that the man recommended visiting the rose garden, so they follow the signs to the *Giardino delle Rose* on the way down.

Panini for lunch

It's lunchtime in Florence, but Sarah and Maria are too busy sightseeing to stop for lunch at a restaurant. When they were heading up to the Piazzale Michelangelo they passed by a popular panini shop that was nothing more than a hole in the wall, but it had a long line. On the way back down they decide to stop at the panini shop for lunch, and just eat on the go.

They are currently queueing and studying the big chalkboard menu with lots of different sandwich options.

Maria: Which sandwich do you want?

Sarah: I don't know, there are so many to choose from, and I don't even understand what half the words mean. I'm looking at the number six, with the *prosciutto crudo*, *mozzarella* and *pomodori secchi*. I know *pomodori* means tomatoes, but what is *secchi*?

Maria: *Secco* means dry, so *pomodori secchi* is sun dried tomatoes.

Sarah: That sounds nice. I might get that if nothing else looks more interesting. On the number seven, what is *tonno* and *acciughe*?

Maria: *Tonno* is tuna, and *acciughe* is anchovies. You could get that, but your breath might not be the best after...

Sarah: Ok, ok I get the hint, no *tonno*. The number nine has *melanzane grigliate*, *cipolla* and *peperoni grigliate*, that sounds nice, I love pepperoni.

Maria: Unfortunately *peperoni* is a bit of a language false friend here, it means bell peppers. So the sandwich has grilled aubergine, onions and grilled bell peppers. Very healthy, but probably not what you wanted?

Sarah: Oh, no that's not what I was after.

Maria: *Salame* is salami, so that's the Italian version of what you're after I think. So you could go for the number three with *salame, lattuga, pomodori freschi* and *pecorino.*

Sarah: That does sound quite nice actually. I'll get the number three. What about you?

Maria: I'm tempted for number four, with the *caprino, pomodori secchi* and *rucola. Caprino* is an Italian goat's cheese I love the flavour of, and *rucola* is rocket salad, which has a bit of a kick to it. It sounds like a nice combination.

Finally, it is Maria and Sarah's turn to order. They step up to the vendor at the small hole-in-the-wall panini shop.

Venditore: Buongiorno! Cosa desiderate?

Sarah: Buongiorno! Due panini, per favore. Numero tre e numero quattro.

Venditore: Certo. Da bere?

Sarah: Una bottiglia di acqua frizzante e una di acqua naturale, per favore.

Venditore: Va bene. Un numero tre con salame, lattuga, pomodori freschi e pecorino. Un numero quattro con caprino, pomodori secchi e rucola. Acqua frizzante e acqua naturale. In totale, quindici euro. Può pure pagare qui, per favore.

Sarah pays €15 by card for their two paninis and waters. The vendor smiles and gestures to the side, where he asks them to wait for five minutes while he makes the paninis.

Venditore: Grazie. Aspettate lì per cinque minuti, mentre preparo i panini.

A few minutes later, the vendor hands them their paninis, which are bursting with fillings.

Venditore: Ecco i vostri panini.

Sarah: Grazie. Sembrano deliziosi!

Sarah takes a big bite of her *panino*, and is so positively surprised by the bursting flavours that she compliments the vendor while still chewing.

Sarah: Squisito!

Maria: Sì, davvero delizioso!

Venditore: Grazie mille!

They take their paninis, and continue strolling through the streets of Florence, enjoying the views and their food.

Visiting a wine window

Walking through the narrow streets of Florence, Maria and Sarah have just finished their paninis. They are enjoying the sights and sounds of the city when they suddenly come across an ancient wine window that's still serving wine. It is no more than a small, arched opening in the middle of the wall, just big enough to pass a glass or bottle of wine through. Outside the window are patrons perching on the pavement, enjoying their glasses and bottles of wine.

Sarah: Oh my god, it's a wine window, a *buchetta del vino*! Florence is famous for them. I saw these online. You go over to the wine glass sized hole in the wall, say what wine you want, and they pass a glass of wine out to you! They are from the late Renaissance in the 1600s, hundreds of years ago, when wine merchants created these windows to avoid having to set up shops and pay taxes. Apparently they were also useful during times of plague and pandemics, as you could pass wine through and avoid face-to-face contact. We have to try it!

Sarah eagerly goes up to the wine window and places an order for two glasses of red wine.

Sarah: Buongiorno! Vorrei due bicchieri di vino rosso della casa, per favore.

Venditrice: Buongiorno! Certo, otto euro, per favore.

Sarah pays for the wine, and a hand passes first one then a second glass of red wine through the hole.

Venditrice: Ecco qui i due bicchieri di vino.

Sarah: Grazie mille!

Sarah grabs the two glasses of wine from the window and hands one to Maria. They sit down on the pavement opposite the window and clink their glasses.

Sarah: Cin cin!

Maria: Cin cin!

Perching on the pavement, they sip their wine and enjoy the unique Florentine experience of drinking from a *buchetta del vino*, marveling at the history and charm of the tradition.

Gelato in Florence

It's a hot and sunny summer day in Florence. After a packed morning of sightseeing, including a very hot walk up a long hill to reach the Piazzale Michelangelo, it's time for gelato. Walking down a narrow street with cute shops, Maria and Sarah discover a local gelateria bursting with flavours. They decide to head inside to cool down with some gelato.

Maria walks up the counter to look at the flavours and place her order.

Donna: Buongiorno. Cosa desidera?

Maria: Buongiorno! Vorrei un piccolo cono con due gusti. Lampone e cocco.

The gelato woman takes a small ice cream cone and fills it with raspberry *sorbetto* and coconut gelato. She hands it to Maria.

Donna: Ecco.

Next, she asks Sarah what kind of gelato she would like.

Donna: Cono o coppetta?

Sarah: Vorrei una coppetta con tre gusti. Nocciola, pesca, e fragola.

The woman takes a small paper cup and fills it with hazelnut gelato, peach *sorbetto* and strawberry *sorbetto.*

Donna: Ecco. In totale, cinque euro.

Sarah hands over five euros, and they find a shady spot to enjoy their *gelati.*

Maria: How is your gelato?

Sarah: Delicious! The double *sorbetti* of peach and strawberries is really refreshing, and the hazelnut gelato is nice and creamy.

Maria: The creamy *cocco* goes really well with the slightly sour *lampone.*

After finishing their *gelati*, they continue exploring Florence.

Jewelry shopping on Ponte Vecchio

Any trip to Florence eventually ends up with a trip across the famous Ponte Vecchio, the old bridge that is lined with jewelry shops on both sides. Maria and Sarah have found their way there, and are browsing the selection of jewelry stores.

Sarah stops in front of a shop with a sign saying *gioielleria*, with a full window display of gold and silver jewelry. There are rings, necklaces and earrings.

Sarah: Come look at this gold necklace, isn't it beautiful?

Maria: Ooo that's nice! I also love the gold earrings next to it.

Sarah: They are very pretty. The silver rings with gemstones are nice too. Should we go in and have a look?

Sarah enters the store, which is tiny on the inside. It looks like the majority of the shop's collection is on display in the window, with just a small counter to try things on in the actual shop. There is an older man behind the counter, who looks up and greets them as they enter.

Gioielliere: Buongiorno! Come posso aiutarvi?

Sarah: Buongiorno! Posso vedere la collana d'oro nella vetrina e anche gli orecchini d'oro accanto?

Gioielliere: Certo. Puoi indicarmeli? Ci sono molti gioielli nella vetrina.

Sarah asks the vendor if she can try on the gold necklace she was looking at in the window, as well as the gold earrings Maria liked next to them. The vendor is happy for her to try them on, but she has to go point them out to him in the window, as the shop window is so crowded with jewellery. Sarah exits the shop, and points at the jewellery she wants to try in the window.

Sarah: Questa collana qui.

Gioielliere: Questa?

The jeweller points at a necklace that is to the right of the necklace that Sarah wants to try on. Sarah helps him out by pointing at the necklace she wants, and tells him it's left of the one he's pointing at.

Sarah: No. Quella accanto, a sinistra.

Gioielliere: Questa?

Sarah: Sì!

Gioielliere: Volete provare anche questa collana d'argento?

Sarah: No, grazie.

After a bit of back and forth in the window the vendor is able to locate the correct necklace. He also asks if Sarah wants to try on a silver necklace, but she politely declines, preferring the gold necklace. Now Sarah excitedly tries on the gold necklace and Maria gold earrings.

Gioielliere: Bellissima!

Sarah: Grazie. Ha uno specchio?

Gioielliere: Sì, prego.

The jeweller tells Sarah she looks beautiful in the necklace. She asks for a mirror, so she can see for herself. When the jeweller hands her the mirror, she admires herself wearing the gold necklace. It really is beautiful on her, and glimmers in the shop lights.

Sarah: Che bella! Quanto costa?

Gioielliere: Costa quattrocentocinquanta euro.

Sarah: È troppo cara per me!

Gioielliere: Posso dartela per quattrocento euro.

When Sarah asks how much the beautiful necklace costs, she is surprised to discover that it costs €450, which is too expensive for her. The jeweller then says something else she doesn't understand about €400, so she looks to Maria to help her with the negotiation, as her Italian vocabulary doesn't yet stretch to haggling.

Sarah: I don't understand what the new price he's offering is?

Maria: He's offering to give it to you for 400 euro instead of 450 euro. Dartelo is a common haggling word, but a bit confusing. It's a combination of dare, which means to give, te, which means to you, and lo, which means it.

Sarah: Ah, thanks for explaining. Fifty euro off 450 is just an 11% discount, not that much. Can you ask if we can get it for 360 euro, so a 20% discount?

Maria turns back to the jeweller to help Sarah haggle for her necklace.

Maria: Che ne dice di trecentosessanta euro?

Gioielliere: Mi dispiace, ma trecentonovanta euro è il prezzo più basso che posso offrire.

Maria: È comunque troppo.

Sarah disappointedly takes off the gold necklace and gives it back to the man. Both the original price of €450 and the discounted offers of €400 and €390 are too expensive for her. Maria takes off her earrings too, realising they'll also be more than she's willing to pay.

Sarah: Grazie, arrivederci.

Gioielliere: Buona giornata.

They continue browsing the window displays of the jewelry shops across the bridge, but don't go in to try on any more jewelry.

Shoe shopping

Florence is filled with cute shops selling clothes, bags and shoes. Sarah stops outside a local shoe store and admires a pair of pretty, yellow shoes in the window. She decides to go inside to try them on.

Sarah: Scusi, posso provare le scarpe gialle in vetrina?

Commesso: Sì, qual è la sua taglia?

Sarah: Trentanove.

Commesso: Un momento, le prendo subito.

The shop assistant disappears into the back, and re-appears a few moments later with a shoe box. He takes out the yellow shoes and gives them to Sarah to try on.

Commesso: Ecco le scarpe. Lo specchio è lì.

Sarah: Grazie.

Sarah puts on the shoes. She goes over to the mirror the shop assistant pointed out and admires how she looks.

Sarah: Mi piacciono molto, ma sono troppo grandi. Posso provare la taglia trentotto?

Commesso: Certo. Ritorno subito.

Since Sarah said the shoes were too big and asked to try them on in a size 38 instead, the shop assistant has gone to fetch the smaller shoes. In the meantime, she has a look around the shop. On a shelf inside the store she finds a pair of blue loafers and a pair of red heels that she would also like to try on.

Commesso: Ecco qui le scarpe in taglia trentotto.

Sarah: Grazie. Posso provare anche questi mocassini blu e queste scarpe rosse con il tacco alto?

Commesso: Certo, un momento.

While the shop assistant goes to look for the blue loafers and the red high heels, Sarah admires herself in the mirror. She likes the yellow shoes, and they fit well in a smaller size. Not long after, the shop assistant returns with four shoe boxes.

Commesso: Allora, ho i mocassini blu in taglia trentotto e trentanove.

He puts two shoe boxes of blue loafers down in front of Sarah. Holding the remaining two boxes, he explains that the high heels are only available in red in a size 37, but he has them in black in size 38.

Commesso: Le scarpe con il tacco sono disponibili solo in taglia trentasette. In alternativa, le ho in nero in taglia trentotto. Vuole provare i tacchi alti rossi in taglia trentasette, o quelli neri in taglia trentotto?

Sarah: Va bene, allora non prendo le scarpe con il tacco.

The shop assistant puts away the two shoe boxes with heels that she does not want, and asks her how she's finding the yellow shoes and the blue loafers.

Commesso: Come le sembrano le scarpe gialle e i mocassini blu?

Sarah: Mi piacciono le scarpe gialle. Quanto costano?

Commesso: Costano quarantacinque euro.

Sarah: Perfetto, le prendo.

Commesso: Ottimo! Venga con me alla cassa.

Sarah: Pago con la carta di credito.

Sarah decides to buy the yellow shoes. They are 45 euro and she pays for them by card. Afterwards, she happily continues down the street, bag with new yellow shoes in hand.

Souvenir shopping

No trip to Florence is complete without some souvenirs to bring back home. Walking down one of the busy tourist streets near Ponte Vecchio, Sarah spots an old looking stationary shop selling pretty notebooks and other stationery that looks artisanal.

Upon entering the stationery shop, Sarah is greeted by a friendly shop assistant who welcomes her with a big smile. The shop assistant lists out some of the things her small shop sells; like notebooks, pens, bookmarks, and postcards. She asks what Sarah is looking for, but Sarah is just having a curious look around the shop.

Commessa: Benvenute! Abbiamo taccuini, penne, segnalibri e cartoline. Cosa sta cercando?

Sarah: Oh, grazie, sto solo dando un'occhiata.

Sarah wanders around the store looking at the artisanal looking products on display. There are postcards and bookmarks with sights from Florence on them, leather bound notebooks, fountain pens, and letter writing sets. Sarah picks up a leather bound notebook, and a postcard with a picture of the city of Florence on it, and heads over to the till.

Sarah: Ciao, vorrei comprare questo taccuino e questa cartolina. Quanto costa il taccuino?

Commessa: Ottima scelta. Il taccuino di pelle viene quindici euro. La cartolina con la città di Firenze viene un euro e cinquanta centesimi. In tutto, sono sedici euro e cinquanta.

Sarah pays €16.50 by card, takes the bag with her purchase, and exits the store.

A few shops down the street, Sarah sees a store selling miscellaneous souvenirs, including little statuettes.

Sarah: We're in Florence, I have to bring back a small David statue!

Maria: Haha, go for it.

Sarah asks the shop assistant for help.

Sarah: Ciao, avete una piccola statuetta del David?

Commesso: Sì, abbiamo statuette in molte dimensioni diverse. Mi segua.

The shop assistant takes her over to a collection of small statuettes, including a few different sizes of David. Sarah picks up a small one.

Sarah: Prendo questa.

Commesso: Perfetto. Vuole qualcos'altro?

Sarah: No, solo la statuetta del David.

As Sarah walks over to the till with her David statuette, she spots some I love Florence t-shirts. She asks the shop assistant if they have the t-shirt in white in a size medium.

Sarah: Scusi, avete questa maglietta bianca nella taglia media?

Commesso: Le magliette bianche sono finite. Però abbiamo lo stesso modello in rosso e nero. Provi la maglietta nera, snellisce. Vado a prenderla.

The shop assistant tells her they are sold out of the medium sized white t-shirt, but they have it in red and black. He tells her that he will fetch her the black one to try on, as it's slimming, and disappears into the back without waiting for her answer. Sarah feels a little offended by the slimming comment. Moments later, he returns with the black t-shirt, which she tells him that she doesn't want.

Sarah: Non la voglio in nero, grazie.

Commesso: Mi dispiace.

Sarah: Prendo solo la statuetta.

Sarah pays for the statuette and exits the shop.

Sarah: Can you believe the shop assistant told me to try on the black t-shirt because it's slimming!

Maria: Ouch. Haha, maybe you've had too many scoops of gelato recently?

Sarah: You can never have too many scoops of Italian gelato when on holiday!

They continue their stroll down the busy street, visiting shops that look interesting.

Dinner in Florence

It's dinner time in Florence, and Maria decides that they should go to a local restaurant and try the famous *bistecca fiorentina*. She has done some research online, and found a cozy restaurant in the centre of town that specialises in the regional steak favourite.

Maria calls ahead to make a reservation, to ensure they get a table for dinner at the popular restaurant.

Cameriere (telefono): Pronto, Bisteccheria Rossa. Come posso aiutarla?

Maria (telefono): Buongiorno. Vorrei prenotare un tavolo per due persone per questa sera, per favore.

Cameriere (telefono): Certo. Abbiamo un tavolo disponibile alle otto. A che nome faccio la prenotazione?

Maria (telefono): Maria Bianchi.

Cameriere (telefono): Benissimo, signora Bianchi. La aspettiamo stasera alle otto.

Maria (telefono): Grazie mille. A stasera.

Maria successfully reserves a table for two at eight o'clock that evening.

When the evening rolls around, they show up hungry and excited to try the local steak speciality. The waiter shows them to their table and hands them their menus.

Sarah: So what is *bistecca fiorentina* anyway?

Maria: *Bistecca fiorentina* is a traditional Tuscan dish, a large T-bone steak that is grilled on charcoal and best served rare or medium rare. It's made from Chianina beef, a local breed known for its tenderness and flavor. To bring out the flavour of the meat it's typically seasoned with just olive oil, salt, and pepper – no sauce. You will usually see it served with side dishes like fagioli beans and roasted potatoes. It's a real must-try if you're in the Florence region!

The waiter comes over to their table to take their order.

Cameriere: Buonasera. Cosa desidera?

Maria: Vorrei una bistecca alla fiorentina, una bottiglia di vino rosso della casa e dell'acqua gassata, per favore.

Cameriere: Come desidera la carne? Noi consigliamo al sangue.

Maria: Cottura media al sangue, per favore.

Cameriere: Va bene. Desidera qualcos'altro?

Maria: No, basta così, grazie.

The waiter disappears to place their order.

Sarah: Why did you only order one steak?

Maria Oh they are over a kilo, with a big bone in, so between the two of us we will probably struggle to finish one. They are so large so they can be properly chargrilled on the outside, but still rare in the middle.

Sarah: That makes sense. I can't wait to try it!

A moment later the waiter returns with their red house wine and sparkling water, and not much later he brings out the big steak they ordered. It's perfectly grilled, with a hint of a smokey flavour from the coal, and medium-rare on the inside.

Sarah: This is delicious! Thank you for bringing me here.

Maria: I'm glad you like it! It really is delicious. They have really mastered the subtle smokey flavour from grilling it on coal. Not every place gets that right.

The waiter comes over to check on them, to see if everything is good.

Cameriere: Tutto bene?

Maria: Sì, è tutto delizioso!

Cameriere: Ottimo!

The waiter disappears again, and they enjoy their steak while chatting about the amazing day they have had in Florence. When they have finished, the waiter comes to take their plates.

Cameriere: Posso?

Sarah: Sí.

The waiter takes their plates, and returns with dessert menus. He asks if they want desserts, but they are simply too full from the giant steak they just ate. Instead, they order two decaf espressos to round off the meal.

Cameriere: Desiderate un dolce?

Maria: No, grazie, siamo piene. Solo due deca, per favore.

Cameriere: Va bene, due deca.

They enjoy their decaf espressos, pay the bill, and take a slow stroll back to the hotel through Florence at night.

Drinks in Florence

Walking back to their hotel in Florence after dinner, Maria and Sarah come across a lively piazza with several packed bars. Since it's their last night in Italy, they decide to make the most of it, and grab one of the last free tables at the most popular-looking bar. They pick up the laminated drinks menu that is standing on their table, and browse the selection.

Sarah: Looks like there are lots of great options here. Wine, cocktails, and beer. Do you know what you want?

Maria: I'm going to have a *Negroni sbagliato*, which has prosecco instead of gin. It's an iconic Italian cocktail. *Sbagliato* means mistake, because legend has it that a bartender mistakenly put prosecco instead of gin into a Negroni, and a new cocktail was born.

Sarah: Love it! I'll have one of those too.

They close their menus, and a few moments later a waiter comes over to take their order.

Cameriere: Buonasera. Cosa desiderate?

Maria: Vorremmo due Negroni sbagliati, per favore.

Cameriere: Ottimo!

The waiter takes their order, and returns shortly afterwards with their drinks. The *Negroni sbagliato* is bright red, and served over ice in a low whiskey glass with a twist of orange.

They are halfway through their first drink when two tall, Italian men sit down at the table next to them. One of the men leans over, introduces himself as Antonio, and asks if he and his friend can buy them a drink, while looking directly at Sarah.

Antonio: Ciao belle, sono Antonio e lui è Luca. Potremmo offrirvi da bere?

Sarah: Volentieri!

Maria: Sì, grazie! Unitevi a noi!

They both happily accept free drinks from the good looking Italian men, and Maria invites them to join their table. With warm smiles, the men move over to Maria and Sarah's table. As soon as Antonio sits down, he signals to the waitress and orders a bottle of Franciacorta for the table.

Antonio: Buonasera. Vorrei una bottiglia di Franciacorta e quattro bicchieri, per favore.

Cameriere: Certo. Ritorno subito.

The waiter returns with a bottle of Franciacorta sparkling wine, and pours four glasses. Antonio raises his glass and toasts the table.

Antonio: Salute, alle nostre nuove amiche!

Tutti: Salute!

Sarah: Parlate inglese?

Antonio: No, dispiace. Solo italiano.

Maria: Non importa, noi parliamo un po' di italiano.

Sarah asks if Antonio and Luca speak English, as her Italian is limited. When the guys say they only speak Italian, Maria says it's fine as she and Sarah speak a little Italian. They try their best to have a simple conversation, and the guys are good at speaking slowly and making themselves understood.

Luca: Siete in vacanza qui?

Maria: Sì, ma partiamo domani.

Antonio: Che peccato!

Luca asks if they are here on vacation, and Maria replies that they are, but are leaving tomorrow, which Antonio exclaims is a pity. Luca goes on to ask where they have been so far, and Maria recounts their trip starting from the seaside, then into Tuscany, and finally ending in Florence.

Luca: Cosa hai visitato finora?

Maria: Siamo state al mare, poi abbiamo girato un po' la Toscana, inclusa Firenze.

Luca: Bello! Abitiamo a Firenze.

Sarah: Vi piacete?

When Luca tells them that they live in Florence, Sarah asks if they like it, and Maria bursts out laughing while the guys look a bit confused. Sarah doesn't understand what's funny, and Maria quickly explains to Sarah what she said in English.

Maria: When you ask if someone likes something in Italian, the pronoun indicates who you are asking, and the verb conjugation indicates who you are asking about. So, if you ask two people if they like pizza, it's a singular object and *vi piace*. If you ask if they like biscuits, it's a plural object and *vi piacciono*. When you ask *vi piacete*, you are using the plural you, asking if they like each other.

Sarah: Oh no!

Sarah looks embarrassed, but laughs it off and asks her questions again, this time in the correct verb tense, and ads on Firenze for extra clarity.

Sarah: Vi piace Firenze?

Antonio: Sì, soprattutto stasera.

Antonio smiles charmingly at Sarah, and says he especially likes Florence tonight. Luca asks them the same question back, and Maria says she likes Florence because it's beautiful and historic. Antonio asks Sarah what her favourite place is in Florence, and she replies the Piazzale Michelangelo, because of its fantastic view.

Luca: E a voi piace Firenze?

Maria: Sì, è bella e storica.

Antonio: Qual è il tuo posto preferito a Firenze?

Sarah: La vista dal Piazzale Michelangelo è fantastica!

They chat through another bottle of Franciacorta in simple Italian, before Maria and Sarah realise it's late and they need to head back to their hotel to catch some sleep before their flight tomorrow.

As Sarah and Maria get up to leave and go back to their hotel, the guys give them a hug and wish them good night.

Antonio: Sarah, posso avere il tuo numero di telefono?

Sarah: Certo, dammi il tuo telefono.

Antonio asks for Sarah's phone number, and Sarah gives it to him by typing it into his phone. He says it was nice to get to know her tonight, Sarah agrees and says she looks forward to his text message.

Antonio: Piacere di averti conosciuta stasera.

Sarah: Anch'io! Aspetto il tuo messaggio.

As they leave, Luca waves goodbye and wishes them a good trip tomorrow. Maria waves back and thanks the guys for the drinks.

Luca: Buon viaggio per domani!

Maria: Grazie per le bevande!

Slowly walking back through the cobbled streets of Florence towards their hotel, they chat while taking in the atmosphere of the city at night.

Sarah: Thank you for teaching me Italian on our holiday. Without your help I would never have been able to speak a bit with Antonio and Luca tonight.

Maria: You're a fast learner! I'm impressed by how quickly you've picked up the language. Do you think you'll continue learning when you get back home?

Sarah: Yes, it would be nice to get better at Italian, so I can more easily hold a conversation the next time I visit Italy.

Maria: I saw you exchanged numbers with Antonio. Do you think you'll stay in touch?

Sarah: Who knows, he doesn't even speak English, and we're leaving tomorrow. If modern dating is anything to go by, I'll probably never hear from him again.

A few minutes later they arrive back at their hotel, and get ready for bed. As Sarah is about to turn out the lights and go to sleep, she gets a text from Antonio.

Antonio (Whatsapp): Buona notte, bella Sarah.

Sarah (Whatsapp): Buona notte, Antonio.

Sarah smiles at her phone, then turns off the lights and goes to sleep.

~ CAPITOLO 6 ~

Last Day in Italy

Leaving Italy

Sarah and Maria have boarded their flight back home, and are sitting next to each other having a chat. Sarah has a window seat, so she can enjoy the view.

Sarah: I've had such a great holiday in Italy! Thank you so much for showing me around, and explaining the Italian language and culture to me. I feel like I've learned so much. *Grazie Mille!*

Maria: It's been my pleasure. I'm so glad you enjoyed our holiday as much as I did.

As their plane takes off, Sarah looks out the window and admires the Italian countryside that's rapidly disappearing below them.

Sarah: *Arrivederci Italia*. I'll be back!

Before You Go

Enjoyed reading?

Ciao!

Thank you for reading! I hope this story filled with the conversations you have on holiday has helped you better understand Italian language and culture. Hopefully, it has inspired you to try speaking Italian the next time you go on holiday to Italy.

If you enjoyed learning with these practical dialogues and situations, visit the CiaoHello Books website at ciaohellobooks.com. On the website you will find more stories, conversation topics, and learning resources to support your Italian language journey.

Arrivederci!
Angie Branaes

Want to use *CiaoHello* books in your classroom?

At *CiaoHello Books*, we are committed to making engaging and relevant language learning materials available to educators and students.

If you want to use *CiaoHello* books for your classroom or tutoring sessions? Visit our education pages at ciaohellobooks.com/education to discover learning resources, educational discounts, and ideas for how you can use our books and stories in your classroom. A great starting point is to have students practice speaking and acting out the dialogues from our stories.

We look forward to hearing from you!
The CiaoHello Books Team

About the Author

Angie Branaes grew up in Norway, lives in England, and spends her summers in Italy. When in Italy, Angie uses her Italian daily, from ordering coffee, to dining out, and shopping at the local markets.

Wanting to make it easy for others to learn the Italian they need to get by, she writes fun and easy-to-read stories that are perfect to read on holiday — or to get excited for an upcoming holiday. Her books emphasize simple, everyday phrases, empowering learners to communicate confidently in any situation, with a view that language is most easily learned when it's experienced and used in context.

Frequently Used Expressions

Below you'll find a summary of common Italian expressions. You can use this as a quick reference to remember the most used phrases.

Greetings

Ciao: Hi/Bye
Buongiorno: Good morning/day
Buonasera: Good evening
Arrivederci: Goodbye
Come stai/sta?: How are you? (informal/formal)
Come va?: How is it going? (informal)
Bene, grazie: Fine, thank you
E tu/Lei?: And you? (informal/formal)

Polite phrases

Grazie: Thank you
Grazie mille: Thanks you very much
Prego: You're welcome
Per favore: Please
Scusa: Excuse me (informal)

Mi scusi: Excuse me / Sorry (formal)
Nessun problema: No problem
Ecco (qui): Here is
Ecco a lei: Here you go
Vorrei ...: I would like
Avete ...: Do you have (polite)
Le andrebbe bene?: Would that work for you? (polite) **La aiuto io**: I'll help her/you (polite)

Questions

Quanto costa?: How much does it cost?
Dov'è ...?: Where is it?
Dove si trova ...?: Where is it located?
Dove si svolge ...?: Where does it take place?
Posso ...?: Can I?
Parli inglese?: Do you speak English?

Restaurant questions

Ha/Avete un prenotazione?: Do you(singular/ plural) have a reservation?
Il conto, per favore: The bill, please
Dov'è il bagno?: Where is the bathroom?
Cosa ci consiglia: What do you recommend (us)?
Avete un tavolo per due?: Do you have a table for two?

Questo piatto è vegetariano?: Is this dish vegetarian?
Quali sono senza latticini/glutine?: Which are dairy/gluten free?
Posso prenotare un tavolo per due alle otto?: Can I reserve a table for two at eight?

Shopping questions

Quanto costa?: How much does it cost?
Posso provare?: Can I try it on?
Dov'è il camerino?: Where is the fitting room?
Avete una taglia più piccola/grande?: Do you have a smaller/larger size?
Avete questo in un'altra taglia?: Do you have this in a different size?
Avete questo in un altro colore?: Do you have this in another color?
È troppo piccolo/grande/caro: It is too small/large/expensive

Grocery phrases

Due etti: Two hectogram (200g)
Mezzo chilo: Half a kilo
Un po' di ...: A little bit of
Dov'è ...: Where is?

Expressing likes/dislikes

Che bello!: How nice!
Va bene: It's fine
Non lo so: I don't know
Mi piace: I like it
Mi dispiace: I'm sorry
Non mi piace/piacciono: I don't like it/them
Ho fame/sete: I'm hungry/thirsty
Delizioso: Delicious
Benissimo: Perfect, very well
Ottimo: Excellent, very good
Perfetto: Perfect

Time

Oggi: Today
Domani: Tomorrow
Ieri: Yesterday
Settimana: Week
Fine settimana: Weekend
Anno: Year

Days of the week

Lunedì: Monday
Martedì: Tuesday
Mercoledì: Wednesday
Giovedì: Thursday
Venerdì: Friday
Sabato: Saturday
Domenica: Sunday

Time expressions

Scorso/a: Last
Questo/a: This
Prossimo/a: Next
Adesso: Now
Poi: Then
Prima: Before
Dopo: After
Sempre: Always
Mai: Never
Spesso: Often
Una volta: Once
A volte: Sometimes
Un momento/attimo: One moment
Aspetta: Wait
Subito: Immediately

Directions

Vai dritto: Go straight
Gira a sinistra: Turn left
Gira a destra: Turn right
Scendi giù: Go down
Salite su: Go up
Torna indietro: Turn back
Qui: Here
Lì: There

Numbers

0: Zero, 1: Uno, 2: Due, 3: Tre, 4: Quattro, 5: Cinque, 6: Sei, 7: Sette, 8: Otto, 9: Nove, 10: Dieci,

11: Undici, 12: Dodici, 13: Tredici, 14: Quattordici, 15: Quindici, 16: Sedici, 17: Diciassette, 18: Diciotto, 19: Diciannove,

20: Venti, 30: Trenta, 40: Quaranta, 50: Cinquanta, 60: Sessanta, 70: Settanta, 80: Ottanta, 90: Novanta,

100: Cento, 1000: Mille.

Ordinals

For ordinals, the ending changes based on the gender of the noun it refers to. This means to say 1st we use **primo** for masculine and **prima** for feminine, and to say 2nd we use **secondo** for masculine and **seconda** for feminine, etc.

Italian Grammar Cheat Sheet

We have included this short Italian grammar cheat sheet to help you get familiar with the essentials of the language. The main thing to remember is that in Italian, we adjust how we say things based on two important factors: the gender of the noun (whether it's masculine or feminine) and whether the noun is singular or plural.

Word order

Word order in Italian is similar to English: **Subject + Verb + Object.** E.g., "Anna mangia una mela." (Anna eats an apple.)

Use subject pronouns sparingly. They are often dropped because the verb indicates the subject. E.g., "Mangio una mela." (I eat an apple.)

Note! Because the subject pronoun often is dropped, misunderstandings can quickly happen if verbs are not conjugated to indicate the right person.

Articles

Italian has definite and indefinite articles (like "the" and "a" in English). These change based on gender, and whether the noun is singular or plural. For example, *il* is used for masculine singular nouns, and *la* is for feminine singular nouns. Like in English, we avoid a double vowel sound, so the articles change to *l'* if the noun starts with a vowel sound.

Definite Articles ("the")

Type	Singular	Plural
Feminine	la casa, l'amica	le case, le amiche
Masculine	il libro, lo studente, l'amico	i libri, gli studenti, gli amici

How to use the masculine definite singular articles:

- **Il** before most consonants (e.g., il libro).
- **L'** before vowels and silent h (e.g., l'amico, l'hotel).
- **Lo** before z/y/z, gn, pn, ps, and s + consonant (e.g., lo zaino, lo studente).

How to use the masculine definite plural articles:

- **i** before most consonants (e.g., i libri)
- **gli** used as the plural article where you use *l'* and *lo* as a singular article (e.g., gli hotel, gli studenti, gli oli).

Indefinite Articles ("a")

Like in English, the indefinite article is only used for singular nouns. Like the definite article, it changes with the gender. For masculine nouns use "un" ("uno" where you use "lo" as a definite article), and for feminine nouns use "una". To avoid a double vowel for feminine nouns, we contract the article (*una* becomes *un'*) with the noun if the noun starts with a vowel (e.g., un'acqua).

Type	Singular
Feminine	una casa, un'amica
Masculine	un libro, uno studente, un amico

Gender of nouns

In Italian, every noun has a gender – either masculine or feminine. There is no neutral gender ("it") in Italian and other latin based languages. You will just have to memorise the gender of the nouns. The easiest way to learn is to consume a lot of Italian content.

The gender of the noun affects the form of other words in the sentence, such as articles and adjectives. For example, il libro (the book) is masculine, while la casa (the house) is feminine. Once you know the gender of a noun, it's easier to use the correct forms of words around it.

Masculine nouns: Usually end in **-o** (e.g., ragazzo) or a consonant (e.g., sport).

Feminine nouns: Usually end in **-a** (e.g., ragazza) or **-ione** (e.g., lezione).

Irregular nouns: Some words are exceptions (e.g., mano is feminine, problema is masculine).

Singular ending	Plural ending
-a	-e
-o, -e	-i

Adjectives

Adjective endings must match the gender and number of the noun they describe. Most adjectives follow the noun (e.g., "una casa grande"), but some common ones (e.g., un bello libro) can come before.

Pronouns

Subject Pronouns

Person	Italian	English
1st singular	io	I
2nd singular informal	tu	you

Person	Italian	English
2nd singular formal	Lei	you (formal)
3rd singular masculine	lui	he
3rd singular feminine	lei	she
1st plural	noi	we
2nd plural	voi	you (plural)
3rd plural	loro	they

Direct object pronouns (Who? What?)
mi, ti, lo/la, ci, vi, li/le Example: Mangi il gelato? Lo mangio. (Are you eating the gelato? I am eating it.) "Lo" is the direct object pronoun in this sentence, because gelato is masculine and singular.

Indirect object pronouns (To whom?)
mi, ti, gli/le, ci, vi, gli
Example: Scrivi a Maria? Sì, le scrivo. (Are you writing to Maria? Yes, I'm writing to her.) "Le" is the indirect object pronoun here, because Maria is feminine and singular.

When to use the formal pronoun "Lei"
Use it with strangers, elderly people, in professional settings, and with people of authority. Example: Lei desidera qualcosa da bere? (Would you like something to drink?), typically asked by a waiter.

Verbs

Italian verbs are grouped into three conjugations based on their endings: **-are, -ere, -ire.**

Regular verbs follow predictable conjugation patterns, as shown in the table below for parlare (to speak), prendere (to take), seguire (to follow):

Person	-are (parlare)	-ere (prendere)	-ire (seguire)
io	parlo	prendo	seguo
tu	parli	prendi	segui
lui/lei	parla	prende	segue
noi	parliamo	prendiamo	seguiamo
voi	parlate	prendete	seguite
loro	parlano	prendono	seguono

Irregular verbs do not follow the regular conjugation patterns. You just have to memorise them. Here are some common irregular verbs:

Verb	Meaning	Conjugation
essere	to be	sono, sei, è, siamo, siete, sono
avere	to have	ho, hai, ha, abbiamo, avete, hanno
fare	to do	faccio, fai, fa, facciamo, fate, fanno
andare	to go	vado, vai, va, andiamo, andate, vanno

Verb	Meaning	Conjugation
venire	to come	vengo, vieni, viene, veniamo, vene, vengono
dire	to say	dico, dici, dice, diciamo, dite, dicono

Modal verbs are used to express ability, necessity, or desire. They are always combined with an infinitive verb. (E.g., Potere: "Posso entrare?" (Can I enter?), Volere: "Voglio mangiare." (I want to eat.))

What are the most common verbs?
Jump to the next chapter to see a convenient summary of the most useful verbs you need to know by heart and their present tense conjugations.

Conjugating the formal "Lei"
In Italian, the formal Lei is conjugated as a 3rd person singular pronoun. E.g., "Lei mangia." (She eats). The easiest way to remember this rule is to think of formal speech as how a butler would speak to you "Would Mr Smith like a cup of tea?".

Reflexive verbs

Reflexive verbs are used when the subject and object of the verb are **the same**. In English, these are often translated with "myself," "yourself," etc. Reflexive verbs always include a reflexive pronoun (**mi, ti, si,**

ci, vi, si) before the verb. You use them as **Reflexive Pronoun + Conjugated Verb**. E.g., "Mi chiamo Maria." (literally: I call myself Maria)

Here is how you'd conjugate the verb Chiamarsi ([pronoun] name is):

Pronoun	**Reflexive pronoun**	**Conjugated verb**
io	mi	chiamo
tu	ti	chiami
lui/lei	si	chiama
noi	ci	chiamiamo
voi	vi	chiamate
loro	si	chiamano

What happens if I forget to add the pronoun when using the reflexive verb?

If you drop the pronoun, the verb switches from being reflexive to being the normal verb. This changes the meaning of the sentence. Let's take chiamare (to call) and chiamarsi (to be called) as an example. Say you are called Maria and are introducing yourself as "Mi chiamo Maria" meaning "I call myself Maria". If you drop the reflexive pronoun "mi" from the sentence and say "chiamo Maria", you are saying "I call Maria", implying that you called a different person called Maria. Sometimes context can save you from confusion if you're lucky, but sometimes it leads to funny misunderstandings.

Verbs with pronouns

Some verbs can combine with direct or indirect object pronouns to indicate "for me," "to you," "for us," etc. The pronoun attaches to the **infinitive**, or stands before a conjugated verb. When attaching the pronoun to the infinitive, drop the final "e". E.g., comprare + mi → comprarmi. This is similar to using the reflexive verb.

- Pronoun before conjugated verb: "**Ti** compro un caffè." (I'm buying you a coffee.).
- Infinitive verb joined with pronoun: "Posso comptriar**ti** un caffè?" (Can I buy you a coffee?)

Pronoun	Meaning	Separate Pronouns Example
mi	to/for me	Mi compri una pizza? (Will you buy me a pizza?)
ti	to/for you	Ti scrivo una lettera. (I'll write you a letter.)
gli/le	to him	Gli porto un regalo. (I'll bring him a gift.)
le	to her	Gli porto un regalo. (I'll bring him a gift.)
ci	to/for us	Ci dai il libro? (Will you give us the book?)
vi	to/for you (pl.)	Vi compro qualcosa. (I'll buy you something.)

Pronoun	Meaning	Separate Pronouns Example
gli	to them	Gli mando un messaggio. (I'll send them a message.)

Pronoun	Meaning	Joined Example
mi	to/for me	Devi comprarmi una pizza. (You have to buy me a pizza.)
ti	to/for you	Voglio scriverti una lettera. (I want to write you a letter.)
gli/le	to him	Puoi portargli un regalo? (Can you bring him a gift?)
le	to her	Devo darle un consiglio. (I have to give her advice.)
ci	to/for us	Potete prestarci la macchina? (Can you lend us the car?)
vi	to/for you (pl.)	Vogliamo mandarvi un messaggio. (We want to send you a message.)
gli	to them	Devi spiegargli il problema. (You have to explain the problem to them.)

Imperative verbs

The imperative mood in Italian is very useful when you're interacting with people in everyday situations; whether you're giving directions, making requests, or offering suggestions. It is used to give commands, requests, advice, or suggestions. It's similar to saying "do something" or "let's do something" in English.

Note that when we use imperative, we don't use the subject pronoun (E.g., we say "Mangia!" instead of "Tu mangia!").

Forming the imperative

For regular verbs, the imperative is formed differently depending on the verb ending (-are, -ere, -ire) and whether the command is informal (tu) or formal (Lei).

-are verbs: Drop the final -re and add -a for "tu" (informal) and -i for "Lei" (formal).

Mangiare (to eat):
- Tu: mangia! (Eat! - informal)
- Lei: mangi! (Eat! - formal)

-ere verbs: Drop the final -re and add -i for "tu" (informal) and -a for "Lei" (formal).

Leggere (to read):
- Tu: leggi! (Read! - informal)
- Lei: legga! (Read! - formal)

-ire verbs: Drop the final -re and add -i for "tu" (informal) and -a for "Lei" (formal).

Dormire (to sleep):
- Tu: dormi! (Sleep! - informal)
- Lei: dorma! (Sleep! - formal)

The “noi” form (let’s...) and the “voi” form (you all...) both use their respective present tense conjugations, e.g., Andiamo! (Let’s go!) and Mangiate! (Eat! - plural).

When using direct or indirect object pronouns (like mi, ti, lo, la, ci, vi) with the imperative, they are attached to the verb. E.g., Guardami! (Look at me!).

Expressing certainty and wishes through verb tenses

Italian has many different verb tenses to wrap your head around, but two of the most used ones for beginners are Present Indicative and Present Conditional. As a beginner, you can get by and be understood knowing only Present Indicative (e.g., Io voglio - I want). As your Italian improves and you become more confident, you can start to introduce the use of polite verb tenses, similar to using “would” in English. You are likely already using the Present Conditional without even realising, as saying “Vorrei un caffè” (I would like a coffee) uses this verb tense of Volere.
- **Present Indicative**: Used to express certainty.

Including talking about facts, habits and things happening in the present. (E.g., Fa caldo oggi - It's hot today.)

- **Present Conditional**: Used to express politeness, wishes and hypothetical situations. Typically where you use "would" in English. (E.g., Vorrei un caffè – I would like a coffee)

Pronoun	Volere - Indicative	Volere - Conditional
io	voglio	vorrei
tu	vuoi	vorresti
lei/lui	vuole	vorrebbe
noi	vogliamo	vorremmo
voi	volcte	vorreste
loro	vogliono	vorrebbero

Common prepositions

Italian	Meaning	Example
a	to, at, in	Vado **a** Roma. (I go to Rome.)
in	in, into, to	Sono **in** Italia. (I am in Italy.)
di	of, from	Un libro **di** Marco. (A book by Marco.)
da	from, since, by	Vengo **da** Milano. (I come from Milan.)

Italian	Meaning	Example
con	with	Esco **con** amici. (I go out with friends.)
su	on, about	Il libro è **su** tavolo. (The book is on the table.)
sopra	on, above	Il libro è **sopra** il tavolo. (The book is above the table.)
sotto	under, below	Il libro è **sotto** il tavolo. (The book is under the table.)
tra/fra	between, among	Il libro è **tra/fra** noi. (The book is between us.)
per	for, through, by	Cammino **per** le strade. (I walk through the streets.)
dietro	behind	Il libro è **dietro** il tavolo. (The book is behind the table.)
davanti	in front of	Il libro è **davanti** al tavolo. (The book is in front of the table.)
intorno	around	Cammino **intorno** al parco. (I walk around the park.)
di fianco	next to	La casa è **di fianco** al parco. (The house is next to the park.)

Using prepositions with articles

In Italian, many prepositions combine with definite articles (il, lo, la, l', i, gli, le). Here's how they work:

Preposition	il	lo	l'	la	i	gli	le
a	al	allo	all'	alla	ai	agli	alle
in	nel	nello	nell'	nella	nei	negli	nelle
di	del	dello	dell'	della	dei	degli	delle
da	dal	dallo	dall'	dalla	dai	dagli	dalle
su	sul	sullo	sull'	sulla	sui	sugli	sulle

Examples:
- al: Vado al mercato. (I go to the market.)
- nel: Vivo nel centro. (I live in the center.)
- del: Il libro del ragazzo. (The boy's book.)
- dallo: Vengo dallo stadio. (I come from the stadium.)
- sul: Il libro è sul tavolo. (The book is on the table.)

When to contract prepositions

Prepositions only contract when they are directly followed by a definite article (e.g., il, la). They do not contract with indefinite articles (e.g., un, una). E.g., "Sono **in una** città." (I am in a city.). Sono **nella** città. (I am in the city.)

When to use "In" vs "A":
- "In" often refers to being inside or within, including countries. E.g., "Vivo **nel** centro." (I live in the center.)
- "A" is used for destinations. E.g., "Vado **al** ristorante." (I go to the restaurant.)

“Di” for possession:
- It functions like ’s in English. E.g., “Il cane **del** ragazzo.” (The boy’s dog.)

What’s next?

Now that you have read through this cheat sheet with the essentials of Italian grammar, read the book one more time and see if you understand more of the Italian dialogue.

Useful Italian Verbs

Learning to conjugate Italian verbs can feel overwelming at first, as there is a lot to remember. To make it easier to get started, we have included the most common present tense conjugations (Present Indicative) for the Italian verbs you'll find yourself using daily.

Regular verbs

-are Verbs

Pronoun	Parlare (to speak)	Mangiare (to eat)
io	parlo	mangio
tu	parli	mangi
lui/lei	parla	mangia
noi	parliamo	mangiamo
voi	parlate	mangiate
loro	parlano	mangiano

-ere Verbs

Pronoun	Sapere (to know)	Prendere (to take)
io	so	prendo

Pronoun	Sapere (to know)	Prendere (to take)
tu	sai	prendi
lui/lei	sa	prende
noi	sappiamo	prendiamo
voi	sapete	prendete
loro	sanno	prendono

-ire Verbs

Pronoun	Finire (to finish)	Partire (to leave)
io	finisco	parto
tu	finisci	parti
lui/lei	finisce	parte
noi	finiamo	partiamo
voi	finite	partite
loro	finiscono	partono

Irregular Verbs

Essere (to be)

io	sono
tu	sei
lui/lei	è
noi	siamo

voi siete

loro sono

Avere (to have)

io ho

tu hai

lui/lei ha

noi abbiamo

voi avete

loro hanno

Fare (to do/make)

io faccio

tu fai

lui/lei fa

noi facciamo

voi fate

loro fanno

Andare (to go)

io vado

tu vai

lui/lei va

noi	andiamo
voi	andate
loro	vanno

Dire (to say)

io	dico
tu	dici
lui/lei	dice
noi	diciamo
voi	dite
loro	dicono

Dare (to give)

io	do
tu	dai
lui/lei	dà
noi	diamo
voi	date
loro	danno

Stare (to stay)

io	sto
tu	stai

lui/lei sta

noi stiamo

voi state

loro stanno

Venire (to come)

io vengo

tu vieni

lui/lei viene

noi veniamo

voi venite

loro vengono

Volere (to want)

io voglio

tu vuoi

lui/lei vuole

noi vogliamo

voi volete

loro vogliono

Vocabulary

A

a bordo aboard, on board

abitare to live, to reside

accanto next to

acciuga anchovies

aceto vinegar

acqua water

acqua naturale still water

acquistare to purchase

addetto/a attendant, staff

addominali abs

agriturismo farm holiday stay

agrume citrus

ai ferri grilled

al sangue rare (steak)

albicocca apricot

alcuno some

alimentari groceries, grocery store

allora so, then

alto tall, high

altro another, other, different

amare love

amarena black cherry

anche also

ancora again

andare to go

anguria watermelon

anni year

antipasto starter, appetizer

aperitivo aperitif, appetizer

aperto open

apprezzato appreciated

arachide peanut

arancia orange (fruit)

argento silver

arrabbiata angry, spicy

arrivare arrive

arrivederci goodbye, see you later

aspetta wait

aspettare to wait for

assaggiare to taste, try, sample

attraverso across

azzurro blue, azure

B

bagaglio luggage

bagno bathroom

barca boat

barcaiolo boatman, hires out boats

basso short, low

basta così enough

bella beautiful

bellezza beauty

bellissima beautiful

bene good

benissimo very well, perfect

benvenuto welcome

bere to drink

bianco white

bicchiere glass, cup

bici bicycle, informal for bicicletta

bicicletta bicycle

biglietto ticket

bisogno need

bistecca steak

bisteccheria steakhouse

bloccare block, stop

blu blue

borsa bag

bosco forest

botte barrel, cask

bottiglia bottle

branzino seabass

brioche brioche, sweet roll, croissant (Northern Italy)

buchetta small hole, small opening

buona serata have a good evening

buonasera good evening

buongiorno good day (literal), good morning

buono good

busta bag

C

caffè coffee

caldo hot

calmo calm

cambiare to change

camera bedroom, room

cameriere/a waiter/ waitress

camerino fitting room

camminare to walk

campagna countryside

campo da tennis tennis court

cantina wine cellar, winery

capire to understand

capitano captain

cappello hat

cappucci short for cappuccini

capra goat

caprino goats cheese, goat

carta card, paper, menu

cartello sign

cartolina postcard

casa house

cattedrale cathedral

cattolico catholic

centro centre,

centro storico old town

certo certainly

che who, which, what, that, than

chiamare to call

chiamarsi to call oneself (reflexive)

chiave key

chiesa church

chilo kilo

chiosco kiosk

ci us

cima top, peak, summit

cin cin cheers

cinghiale wild boar

cinquanta fifty

cioccolato chocolate

cipolla onion

circa about, around

città city, town

cocco coconut

colazione breakfast

collana necklace

collina hill

coltivare to cultivate, to grow

come how

commesso/a shop assistant

comprare to buy

comunque anyway, in any case

con with

condividere to share

cono cone

consigliare to recommend

consiglio advice, suggestion, recommendation

contante cash

conto bill, check

contorno side dish

controllare to check

controllore ticket inspector

coppetta cup (for gelato)

cornetto croissant, brioche, sweet bun

corridoio corridor, aisle

costa costs

costare to cost

costume da bagno swimsuit

cotoletta breaded cutlet

cotto cooked

cozza mussel

credito credit

crema cream, custard

crema solare sunscreen

crosta crust

crudo raw, cured

cucchiaino teaspoon

cucchiaio spoon

D

dando un'occhiata taking a look

dare to give

dartelo give it to you

dartelo/a dare (to give) + te (to you) + lo/a (it)

davvero really

deca decaf

degustare to taste, to sample

degustazione tasting

delicato delicate, soft, light

delizioso delicious

dentifricio toothpaste

destra right

devi must

dieci ten

dimenticare to forget, to leave behind

dimmi tell me

dire to say

dispiacere be sorry

disponibile available

disponibilità availability

diverso different

documento document

dolce sweet, dessert

domani tomorrow

donna woman

dopo after, later

dove where

dovere must, have to

dritto straight

due two

duomo cathedral, major church

E

e and

ecco here

ecco qui here is, here we are, here you go

esatto exactly

esitare to hesitate

esperienza experience

essere to be (permanent states, characteristics)

estate summer

esterno outside

etto hectogram (100 gram)

F

famoso famous

fantastica fantastic

fare to make, do, be

fattore factor

fenicottero flamingo

festa festival, party, holiday

filetto fillet

finito finished

finora so far

fiore flower, blossom

formaggio cheese

forte strong

forza strength

fragola strawberry

frantoio olive press, olive oil mill

freddo cold

fresco fresh

fritto fried

fritto misto mixed fried fish

frizzante sparkling, bubbly

frutta fruit, fruits

fruttato fruity

frutti di bosco mixed berries, fruits of the forest

frutti di mare seafood (lit. fruits of the sea)

fruttivendolo fruit and vegetable shop

frutto fruit (individual fruits)

fuori outside

G

gamberi prawns

gassata carbonated

gelateria ice cream shop

gelato ice cream

giallo yellow

gioielleria jewelry store

gioielliere/a jeweler

giornata day

giorno day

girare to turn, to rotate

girate turn

giro round trip, tour (visiting multiple places), circle

gita trip, outing, excursion

giubbotto jacket, vest

giubbotto di salvataggio life vest

già already

giù down, downward

gonfiabile inflatable

granchio crab

grande big

grazie thank you

guardare to look at

guida guide

gusto flavour

I

identità identity

impaccare package, wrap

incluso included

incrocio intersection

insalata salad

invece instead, on the other hand

isola island

L

lampone raspberry

lasciare to leave

latte milk

lattuga lettuce

lei she, formal you

lettino beach lounger, beach bed

letto bed

limone lemon

lo it, him

locale local

lui he, him

là there

lì there

M

maglietta t-shirt

mano hand

mare sea

marmellata jam, marmalade

marmo marble

massaggiatrice masseuse

massaggio massage

mattino/a morning

medievale medieval

medio medium

medio al sangue medium rare (steak)

melanzane aubergine, eggplant

melone melon, cantaloupe

mentre while

meraviglioso wonderful, marvellous

metro metre

mettere to put

mezz'ora half an hour

mezzo half

migliore better, best

misto mixed

mocassino moccasin, loafer

modello model, type

molto very

momento moment

mondo world

mora blackberry

morbido soft

muscolo muscle

N

nero black

nessuno no, not any, none

niente nothing

nocciola hazelnut

noce walnut

noleggiare to rent

noleggio rental

nome name

non not

non importa it's not important

nonno grandpa

nostro our

notte night

nuotare to swim

nuoto swimming

nuovo new

O

o or

occhiata a look, a glance, a peek

offerto courtesy of

offrire offer, give

oggi today

ogni every

oleario oil

olio oil

olio d'oliva olive oil

oliva olive

ombrellone beach ubrella

onda wave

opera work, piece

opera d'arte work of art, masterpiece

ora hour, now

orecchino earring

oro gold

ottimo excellent

P

paese village, town

paga pay

pagare to pay

paglia straw

pagnotta loaf

palla ball

pancia belly

pane bread

panetteria bakery

panettiere baker

panino sandwich

panoramica panoramic

partire to leave, to depart

passaporto passport

passare to pass

pasto meal

patatine potato chips, crisps

pausa break

peccato pity, shame

pelle leather

penna pen

peperoni bell peppers

perfetto perfect

però but, however

pesante heavy

pesare weigh

pesca peach

pesce fish

pesce spada swordfish

pezzo piece

piacere to like

piazza town square

piazzale large piazza

piccolo small

pieno full, filled

piscina pool

più more

poi then, after

pomeriggio afternoon

pomodoro tomato

ponte bridge

pontile small pier for docking boats

portare to bring, to deliver

POS card machine

possibile possible

posto place

potere to be able, can

pranzare to have lunch

pranzo lunch

prego you're welcome

prendere to take

prendere il sole sunbathe

prenotare to reserve, to book

prenotazione reservation

preso taken, occupied

prezzo price

primo first

privato private

problema problem

prodotto product

pronto ready, prepared

prosciutto ham

prosciutto crudo dry cured ham

prossimo next

provare to try

pure please, also, too

Q

qualcosa anything, something

qualità quality

quando when

quanto how much

quasi almost

quello that

questo this

qui here, now

R

remo oar

resto rest, remainder, change

retrogusto aftertaste

rilassante relaxing

rilassare to relax

ripiena stuffed, filled

ritiro pick up, collection

ritornare to return

ritorno return

rosa pink

rosso red

rucola rocket, arugula

S

sacchetto bag

salame salami, cold cuts

salato savoury, salty, salted

salire to climb, to go up

salume cured meats, cold cuts

salumeria delicatessen

salute health, cheers

salvataggio rescue, saving

santo holy

sapere to know, to smell/taste like, to seem

sapore flavour, taste

sbagliato wrong, mistaken

scarpa shoe

scelta choice, decision

scoglio rock

scolpire to sculpt

scusi excuse me

scusi/a sorry, pardon me

sdraio beach chair, deckchair

se if

secco dry

seconda casa second house, holiday home

secondo second

sedersi to sit down

sedici sixteen

segnalibro bookmark

seguire follow

sei six

sembrare to seem, to look like

sempre always

seppia cuttlefish

sera evening

serata evening

sette seven

shakerare to shake

simbolo symbol

sinistra left

snellisce slim down

sollevare to lift, to pick up

solo only

sopra up, above, on, over

soprattutto especially, above all

sorbetto sorbet

spazzolino toothbrush

specchio mirror

specialità specialty

spiaggia beach

squisito exquisite, delicious, lovely

stanza room

stare to be (temporary states, conditions or feelings)

stasera tonight, this evening

statuetta small statue, figurine

storico historic

strada street

stuzzichino snack, canapé, finger food

su up, on

sua your, his, her

subito immediately, right away

SUP stand up paddleboard

T

tacco heel

taccuino notebook

taglia size

tanto a lot

tappa stop, landmark, phase

tassametro taxi meter

tavola a table (abstract)

tavolo a table (a physical table)

telefono telephone

telo mare beach towel

tempo time, weather

tipico typical

tipo types, kinds

tonno tuna

tornare to return, to go back

totale total

tra in, between

tra cui including

traghetto ferry

tramezzino small triangle sandwich

tramonto sunset

tranquillo peaceful, tranquil

trattoria traditional Italian restaurant

treno train

trenta thirty

troppo too

trovare to find

tuffarsi to dive

tutti everone

tutto all, everything

U

ultimo final, last

undici eleven

unire join

uomo man

usare to use

uscire exit

uva grape

V

vacanza holiday

valigia suitcase

vaniglia vanilla

vecchio old

vedere to see

venditore male vendor

venditrice female vendor

venire to come

venti twenty

ventitré 23

vento wind

verde green

verdura vegetable

vergine virgin

vero true, real, right

vestito dress, clothing

vetrina shop window, shop display

viaggio trip, journey, travel

vicino nearby, close by

vin santo Vin Santo, dessert wine

vino wine

viso face

vista view

visto che since, given that

vitello veal, calf

vivo alive

volentieri gladly, willingly

volere to want

vostro your

Z

zucchero sugar

zuppa soup

www.ingramcontent.com/pod-product-compliance
Lightning Source LLC
La Vergne TN
LVHW101918220826
846093LV00009B/293

9781068335204